*Drive and Stroll in*

# Norfolk

Anita Delf and
Marilyn Taylor

COUNTRYSIDE BOOKS
NEWBURY BERKSHIRE

First published 2009
© Anita Delf and Marilyn Taylor 2009

All rights reserved. No reproduction
permitted without the prior permission
of the publisher:

COUNTRYSIDE BOOKS
3 Catherine Road
Newbury, Berkshire

To view our complete range of books,
please visit us at
www.countrysidebooks.co.uk

ISBN 978 1 84674 143 2

The cover picture of Beeston supplied by Mike Cowen, Pictures of Britain.

Photographs by Marilyn Taylor
Designed by Peter Davies, Nautilus Design

Produced through MRM Associates Ltd., Reading
Typeset by Mac Style, Beverley, East Yorkshire
Printed in Thailand

# Contents

**Introduction** .................................... 6

| | | |
|---|---|---|
| **Walk 1** | Thornham (4 miles) | .7 |
| **Walk 2** | Sheringham and Beeston Regis (3¼ miles) | .12 |
| **Walk 3** | North Creake (4¼ miles) | .17 |
| **Walk 4** | Around Gunthorpe (4 miles) | .21 |
| **Walk 5** | Paston Great Barn (3½ miles) | .26 |
| **Walk 6** | Heydon and Salle (3 miles) | .31 |
| **Walk 7** | Congham (2½ miles) | .36 |
| **Walk 8** | Whissonsett (3 miles) | .41 |
| **Walk 9** | Horsey Gap (5 miles) | .46 |
| **Walk 10** | Neatishead (2¾ miles) | .50 |
| **Walk 11** | Lyng and Elsing (4 miles) | .54 |
| **Walk 12** | Walpole St Peter and Walpole St Andrew (4½ miles) | .58 |
| **Walk 13** | Pentney Priory (3¼ miles) | .62 |
| **Walk 14** | Around Blofield and Braydeston (3¼ miles) | .67 |

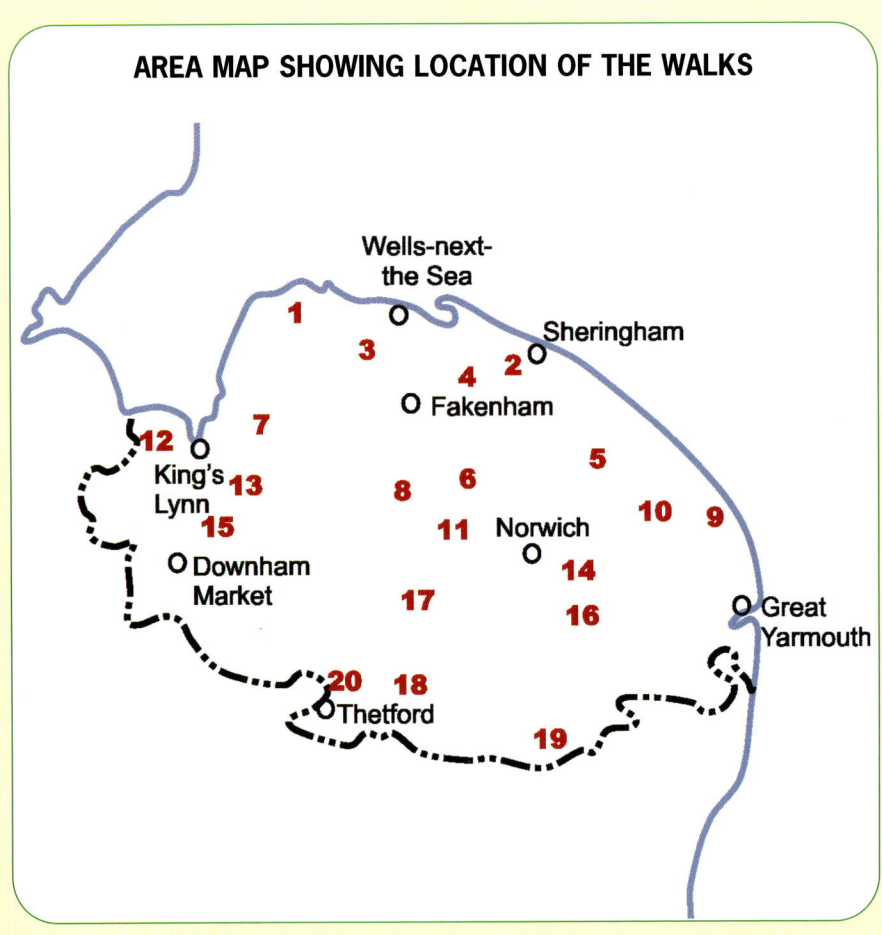

# Contents

| | | |
|---|---|---|
| **Walk 15** | Barton Bendish (3½ miles) | .................71 |
| **Walk 16** | Rockland St Mary (4 miles) | ................75 |
| **Walk 17** | Hingham and Hardingham (5 miles) | ...........79 |
| **Walk 18** | Kenninghall (2¼ miles) | ....................83 |
| **Walk 19** | The Pulhams (4 miles) | ....................87 |
| **Walk 20** | Thetford (2 miles) | .......................92 |

## PUBLISHER'S NOTE

We hope that you obtain considerable enjoyment from this book; great care has been taken in its preparation. Although at the time of publication all routes followed public rights of way or permitted paths, diversion orders can be made and permissions withdrawn.

We cannot, of course, be held responsible for such diversion orders and any inaccuracies in the text which result from these or any other changes to the routes nor any damage which might result from walkers trespassing on private property. We are anxious though that all details covering the walks are kept up to date and would therefore welcome information from readers which would be relevant to future editions.

The simple sketch maps that accompany the walks in this book are based on notes made by the author whilst checking out the routes on the ground. They are designed to show you how to reach the start, to point out the main features of the overall circuit and they contain a progression of numbers that relate to the paragraphs of the text.

However, for the benefit of a proper map, we do recommend that you purchase the relevant Ordnance Survey sheet covering your walk. The Ordnance Survey maps are widely available, especially through booksellers and local newsagents.

# Introduction

These strolls, set in the varied, interesting and beautiful Norfolk countryside, are for people who would like to experience it at close hand. We have included a recommended refreshment stop with each walk for those who, like us, enjoy indulging in morning coffee, lunch, afternoon tea, or even an evening dinner with their outing. These establishments are all of a very high standard and add immeasurably to the enjoyment of the routes. Telephone numbers are given should you wish to book ahead or check availability. For those who would rather defray the cost of refreshment, there is always somewhere you can take a break, admire the view and enjoy a picnic.

If you still have time and energy to spare after your walk, we have suggested places of interest nearby, together with their contact telephone numbers, if applicable, so you can check opening times and admission prices. The walk directions are also accompanied by snippets of information to add to your enjoyment.

The majority of the routes are accessible by public transport but this can be limited in rural areas and timetables tend to change with the seasons. The following telephone numbers should be able to supply details of the services available: First Eastern Bus Company, 01603 788308; National Express Railways 0845 700 7245.

All the walks are suitable for a family outing, with the possible exception of the one at Beeston where part of the cliff end is unfenced, but it goes without saying that adult supervision is required on all routes, especially when close to open water or farm machinery. The use of walking boots is recommended as the paths can be wet and muddy, depending on the season. It is also sensible to take a waterproof and a bottle of water, especially when the weather is hot, and carrying the relevant Ordnance Survey map will greatly add to the enjoyment of your walk.

We have had enormous fun, much pleasure and many cups of tea devising these routes – we hope you find them equally enjoyable.

Happy walking!

*Anita Delf and Marilyn Taylor*

# 1 | Thornham

*Thornham's wonderful landscape*

**Distance:** 4 miles
**Terrain:** Level coastal path, country lanes, one uphill lane
**Map:** OS Explorer 23 Norfolk Coast West, King's Lynn & Hunstanton (GR TF726443)

## How to get there

Thornham is on the A149, 4 miles east of Hunstanton, between the villages of Holme-next-the-Sea and Brancaster. Turn off the road at the western end of the village into Staithe Lane, signposted to the car park and the Lifeboat Inn. Continue, heading seaward, to the very end where the lane peters out. **Parking**: At the car park (please note the warning signs of tidal flooding on this lane and, if necessary, park in the village and follow the coastal path; this goes beside the lane and leads to the starting point of the walk.)

# Drive and Stroll

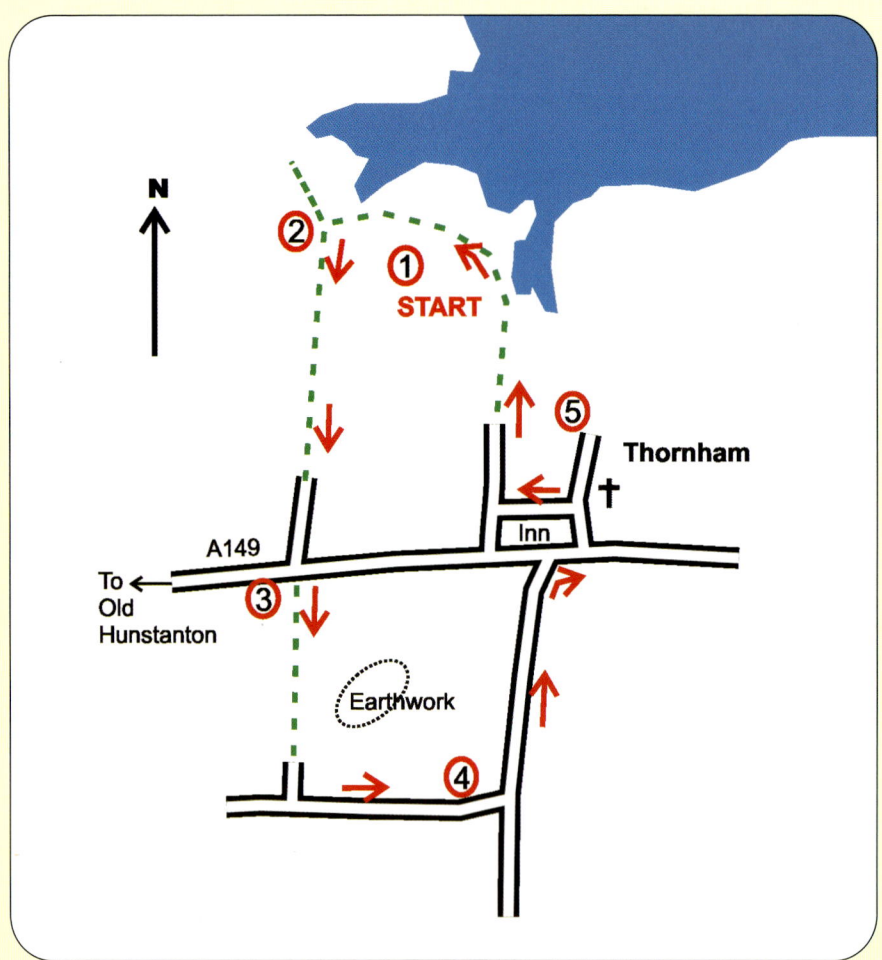

## Introduction
**Thornham is a very special place** for a walk, whether you visit in the quiet of a winter's day or the hot bustle of summer; the fabulous views of the marshes, dunes and the sea beyond are a sheer joy. The walk begins at the Staithe, going along the Coastal Path and Holme Dunes Nature Reserve, then turns inland to climb towards Beacon Hill giving superb views of this beautiful and atmospheric coastline. It returns by lanes passing the parish church and pretty cottages and finally the stupendous Lifeboat Inn before walking the short distance back to the start.

# 1 Thornham

## Refreshments

The **Lifeboat Inn** is a fabulous pub looking out to the coastline and offering any manner of drinks and meals each day throughout the year. Part of it dates from the 16th century when it was an alehouse. There is a large hall entrance, complete with a huge log fire, very welcome after a chilly winter walk, and other smaller bars, together with a conservatory and outside seating for summer evenings. The inn is a treat not to be missed! Telephone: 01485 512236.

## THE WALK

Leave the car park by the track on the left, heading for the information board for the **Holme Dune National Nature Reserve**.

*The reserve is owned and managed by the Norfolk Wildlife Trust, the area being part of the North Norfolk Sites of Special Scientific Interest. The natterjack toad, a rare amphibian, breeds here. This part of the coastline is of international importance for birds in all seasons and the information board lists more details of these.*

Continue over the wooden footbridge between two deep flood pools, turn right from the bridge onto the embankment and continue ahead on the coastal path.

*It is not difficult to imagine, as you look towards the marshes, creeks and the sea, that this was the haunt of smugglers in the 18th and early 19th centuries. Contraband goods included wool, tea, liquor and tobacco. It is recorded that in Thornham four hundredweight of tea was found buried by excise officers in 1783.*

Follow the path to reach a gate marked 'Thornham Parish Wildfowlers', and a three-way signpost. Do not go through the gate but turn left, down the bank, signposted as a public footpath, and go ahead passing a concrete gun emplacement on the left. Follow the clearly marked path as it heads away from the sea; a dyke runs alongside the path and the parish church of Holme-next-the-Sea can be seen to the right.

*It was at the beach near Holme-next-the-Sea that the 4,000-year-old timber circle, known as 'Sea-henge' was sited. Its existence was made public in January 1999, together with the knowledge that it was endangered by the work of the sea. The subsequent removal of what*

# Drive and Stroll

*many felt to be a religious site of the Bronze Age caused much controversy. The treated timbers are now in the Lynn Museum in King's Lynn.*

Immediately after the path bends left, take the right turn at the earth-bridge across the dyke. Continue on the path as it runs alongside a wire fence and woodland; this stretch is liable to flooding and may be very muddy in wet weather. The path eventually turns left over a plank bridge and then swings right. Continue to follow it, going between the double row of trees to reach a five-barred gate and footpath sign. Go around the gate and maintain direction along the lane to the main road ahead.

*One of the many inlets around the coastline*

Cross this very busy road with great care, going left and then immediately right into the narrow lane ahead. Go ahead up this lane, which has little traffic, to reach a T-junction at the top with a trig point on the left.

*As you go up this lane, look behind you at intervals to the splendid view of the coast and sea, including the off-shore wind farm.*

Turn left at the junction and continue along the minor road.

*There are gaps in the hedge affording more spectacular views of the coast and then of the large historical earthworks on the left; to the right is Beacon Hill.*

At the next T-junction turn left, signposted Thornham, and follow this to enter the village, passing **Manor Farm** on the left. Turn right onto the **High Street** and walk ahead passing **The Orange Tree** on the left to reach the parish church. Cross the road to enter the churchyard.

# 1 Thornham

The 20th-century lych-gate was donated by the daughter of Nathaniel Woods; Woods was the last merchant to enter the port on business in 1914, sailing the two-masted cargo boat Jessie May. All Saints church itself is approached by a path flanked with immaculately cut yew trees. Inside, where information leaflets are available, you will find the nave is wider and taller than the typical village church.

Retrace your steps back to the road. Turn right, then right again into **Church Street**, passing some attractive and interesting cottages, including those set back, dated 1682.

Turn left into **Ship Lane**. Go ahead, passing the **Lifeboat Inn**, to the end of the lane, the right turn leading back to the car park. It is possible about halfway along on the left, to take the footpath, rather than the poorly maintained roadway. Continue on the footpath as it bends until you are able to turn right and via the embankment and bridge used previously return to the car park.

### Place of interest nearby

The **Norfolk Wildlife Trust** has a small visitors' centre just a short distance from Thornham, through the next village of Holme-next-the-Sea. It has information, displays, books, gifts and refreshments, as well as bird watching facilities. Follow the A149 towards Hunstanton and the centre is signposted off it; parking is in the NWT car park. The centre has seasonal opening times: telephone 01485 525240.

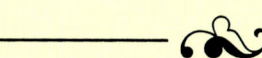

## Drive and Stroll

# 2 | Sheringham and Beeston Regis

*On the beach at Sheringham*

**Distance** 3¼ miles
**Terrain**: Partly level footpaths but with a sizeable climb up and over the hill at Beeston, where an area of cliff edge is unfenced. The walk also crosses the railway line. We consider this walk to be unsuitable for very young children, while older children should have careful supervision.
**Map**: OS Landranger 133. North East Norfolk, Cromer & Wroxham (GR TG158438).

## How to get there

Sheringham is on the A149 coastal road, 4 miles west of Cromer. Turn into the main High Street as directed by the road signs; this narrows and becomes a one-way street. Continue along as it bends right by the sea front to reach the Chequers Pay & Display car park. **Parking:** The town is a popular holiday destination and if the Chequers car park is full, you may be required to park elsewhere and walk to Lifeboat Plain, the start of the walk.

# 2  Sheringham and Beeston Regis

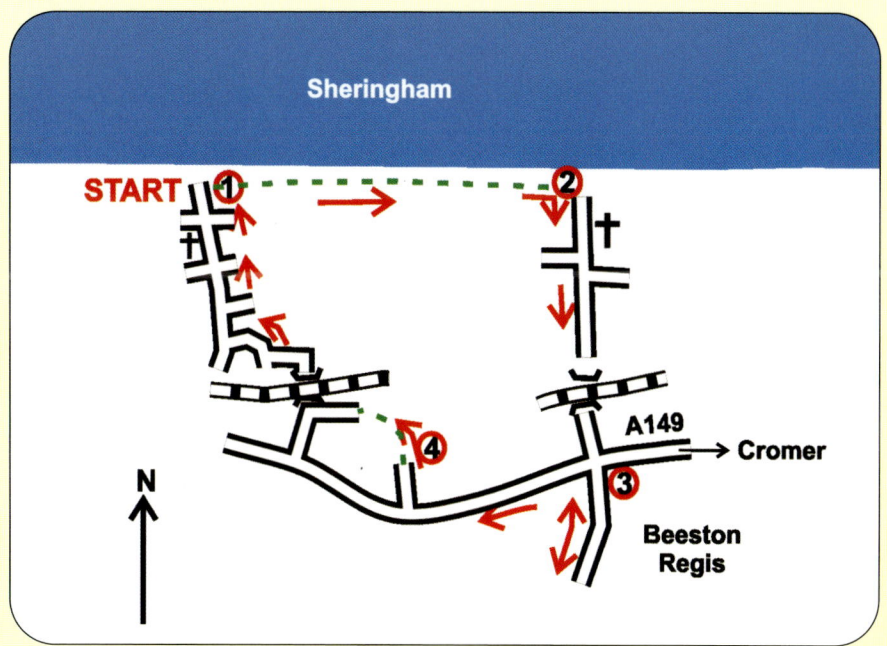

## Introduction
**Beeston Regis is** within an Area of Outstanding Natural Beauty. Unusually for Norfolk, the route incorporates a hill, known as Beeston Bump. Formed by retreating ice at the end of the Ice Age, it affords wonderful panoramic views. The walk begins in Sheringham before climbing the hill, passing a nature trail, then crossing the train track. The walk rises again to Beeston Regis Heath before returning by footpath and lanes to pass the ruins of Beeston Priory and thence to Sheringham and the start.

## Refreshments
Sample the delights of the **Foxglove Tearoom** at Priory Maze, positioned at a strategic point on the walk for refreshment. In addition to the Scandinavian-style log cabin, there is a large tea garden, with chairs, sofas and huge sunshades for a summer's day afternoon tea. The tearoom opens daily offering snacks, as well as more substantial meals. Telephone: 01263 822986.

# Drive and Stroll

## THE WALK

Turn right from the car park into **Lifeboat Plain**, passing **Ye Olde Tea Rooms** on the right. Turn left, go down the slope between concrete bollards, then left again to the promenade, where you turn right. Continue ahead for 300 yards, passing the amusing mural and enjoying the sea view to the left.

*The mural is a reminder of the once important fishing industry here. Today Sheringham is known and loved by day-trippers and holidaymakers.*

Turn right up the flight of steps and continue ahead. At the footpath sign with the acorn emblem, turn left.

*The acorn sign refers to the long-distance coastal path running from Hunstanton in West Norfolk to Cromer, a few miles further east.*

Continue ahead on the well-trodden route, passing several invitingly-placed benches, to reach the steps leading up to the top. It is quite a climb, especially on a windy day, but well worth it for the tremendous views seen from the top.

*The seats at the top are placed to give a terrific panoramic view of Sheringham town, the sea and Beeston church, nestled behind a large caravan site. In the churchyard is a memorial to the legendary boxer, Jem Mace, born in 1831, whose father was the village blacksmith. He became heavyweight champion of England when boxing matches had no time limits; in America one fight lasted 44 rounds!*

Follow the path as it descends by means of further steps. Maintain direction passing to the right of one of a series of display boards showing a nature trail through the open area on the right.

The caravan park lies ahead but the path turns sharp right by the fingerpost with a yellow arrow and an acorn sign. Continue on the path, passing more nature trail boards to arrive at the railway track. Cross the track with care and continue along the stony lane to reach the main road.

Cross this busy road with care and turn left along it for a short distance to the track ahead. Go ahead on the track, this is still the coastal path. Almost immediately bear to the right, still following the path and passing the farm on the left and

# 2  Sheringham and Beeston Regis

*The promenade is just the place for a saunter*

paddocks on the right. The track rises upwards towards woods and eventually reaches **Beeston Regis Heath**. There are more tracks here to explore if you have time.

*The heath covers 30 acres and is managed by the National Trust.*

To resume the walk, retrace your steps back to the main road and turn left. Continue past housing on the left until the sign for the **Priory Gardens** appears on the right. Cross the road to visit the **Foxglove Tearoom**.

*The tearoom is part of the Priory Maze Gardens and an information leaflet states that the 'design and size of the Priory Maze is based on the ruins of the adjacent Beeston*

15

# Drive and Stroll

*Priory'. An entrance fee is payable to visit these lovely gardens.*

From the gardens turn left, walking on the wide grass verge. After 50 yards turn left again along a shingle drive, signed to the abbey ruins.

Take the hedged path to the left. A few yards along the drive, there is an N.C.C. Restricted Byway sign; continue ahead to reach the remains of the priory.

*The ruins come as a surprise as they are invisible from the road and are more majestic than expected. Beeston Priory was founded circa 1216, by Margaret de Cressy. There are excellent information boards within the ruins.*

Continue on the footpath, then after 200 yards pass through a wooden double gate. Turn left and go ahead passing pretty cottages on the right and an area of common to the left. Cross over a small stream then, on reaching the minor lane, turn right going under the railway bridge. Continue ahead on the minor road, then after 200 yards turn left onto a narrow tarmac lane going diagonally left. Go ahead around the metal barriers and continue on the narrow concrete path with a small stream on the left to reach **Priory Road**. Cross the road, turning left and then immediately right onto **Beeston Road**. Continue along the road, passing **Cliff Road** on the right. Maintain direction ahead to arrive back at **Lifeboat Plain** and the start of the walk.

### Place of interest nearby

Within walking distance of Lifeboat Plain, at the end of the High Street is the terminus for the **North Norfolk Railway**. This highly successful line runs through the lovely countryside visiting the restored station at Weybourne and Kelling Halt. Steam engines are frequently used on this line which operates throughout the year. A museum and shop are located within the station which has a large car park. Telephone: 01263 820800; talking timetable 01263 820808.

# North Creake

## 3 | North Creake

*Meadow paths along the way*

**Distance:** 4¼ miles
**Terrain**: Undulating footpaths and country lanes
**Map:** OS Explorer 251, Norfolk Coast Central (GR TF855377)

### How to get there

North Creake is on the B1355, 3 miles south of Burnham Market on the A149 coastal road. **Parking:** In the lay-by on the B1355 opposite the parish church of St Mary the Virgin.

# Drive and Stroll

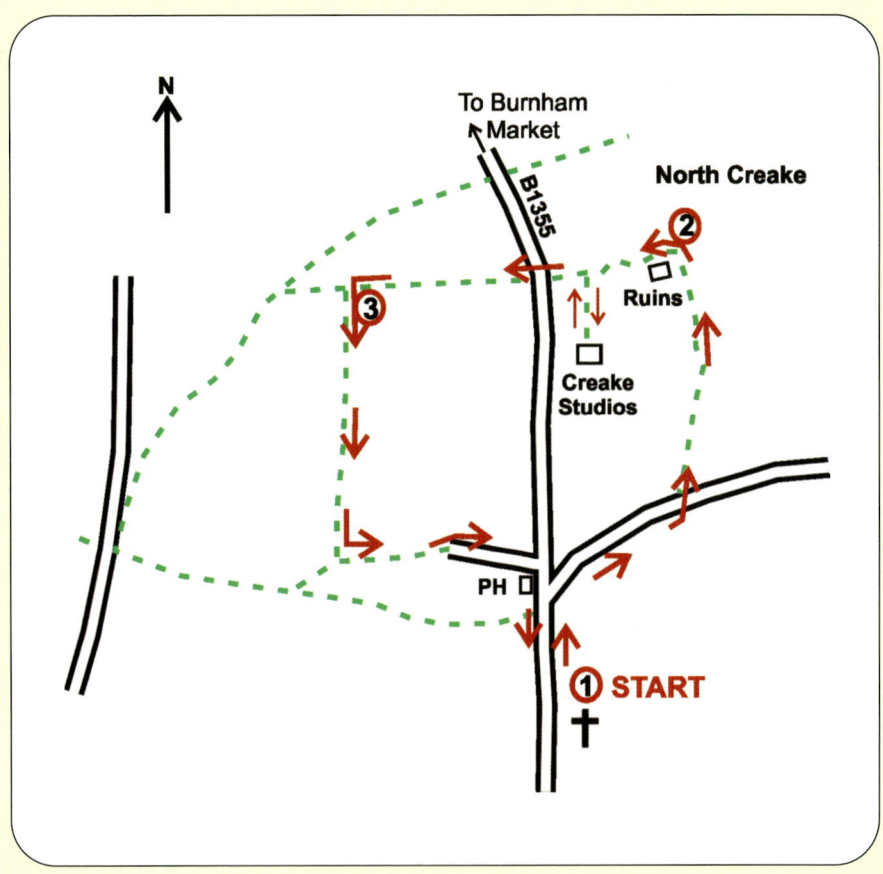

## Introduction
**This very pleasant walk** via footpaths and lanes takes you through the village of North Creake to the picturesque ruins of Creake Abbey, before returning through fields with their commanding views of the undulating countryside.

## Refreshments
**Creake Abbey Studios** is a pretty complex of specialist units housing artists, jewellers, designers and the like. It includes a fabulous coffee shop where a light lunch, cream tea or cake can be enjoyed. Telephone: 07801 418907.

# North Creake

## THE WALK

If you visit the church at the beginning of the walk turn right out of the church grounds, otherwise go north along **Church Street**.

*St Mary the Virgin church has a fine interior with a grand 15th-century hammer beam roof in the nave. The porch and doorway date from about 1300. There is an excellent information leaflet inside.*

Continue ahead passing the school on your right and the village sign on your left.

*The sign depicts the arch of Creake Abbey, the ruins of which will be seen later on the walk. The blacksmith and horses ploughing have now gone but of course the church remains. The sign was made by Roy Masters and erected in 1998.*

Where the road forks, take the right-hand fork along **Wells Road**.

*Look on the left for a plaque set in a stone wall. Unveiled in 2004, this marks a tragic event 60 years earlier when two young men on a night training exercise on 27th April 1944 crashed nearby in their Mosquito fighter aeroplane and were killed. They were both just 23 years of age.*

Continue along the road passing pretty cottages, then just before the road bends sharply to the right, turn left along a wide green track flanked by hedgerows. Gaps in the hedges allow for marvellous views to be seen in this idyllic spot. Go ahead on the footpath, a pale pink-washed farmhouse can eventually be seen, and just before you get there the ruins of Creake Abbey spring into view on the left.

At the end of the path turn left along the lane.

*These unexpected but impressive ruins are in the care of English Heritage and there is no charge for admittance. The abbey was founded in the 12th century as a hospital and almshouse but became an Augustinian priory in 1206. It was largely destroyed by fire in 1484 and in 1506 it was dissolved following the deaths, probably from plague, of the community of monks.*

Continue to the tarmac lane and turn left at the sign to visit **Creake Abbey Studios**, otherwise go ahead to the road. Cross over and go along the track opposite, signposted to **Crossroads Farm**.

# Drive and Stroll

*The ruins of Creake Abbey*

↰ ③

Maintain direction along this sandy lane. As the track rises slightly look carefully for a field with a wide opening on the left and turn here. (There is no footpath sign here.)

*There are wonderful views across the fields to the left and right.*

This becomes an excellent wide track that leads gradually uphill to join a green lane. Turn left and continue to a tarmac road. Maintain direction past the park and houses to reach the main road. Turn right, passing the **Jolly Farmers public house** on the right, to return to the start of the walk.

## Place of interest nearby

Return to Burnham Market and travel east on the A149 to reach the car park for **Holkham Nature Reserve** on the left at Lady Anne Road, directly opposite the entrance to Holkham Hall. Take the boardwalk to the outstanding beach of Holkham and explore the pinewoods, marshes and creeks spread out on either side. It is open all year. If you have any time left, you can add a visit to the Hall!

# 4 Around Gunthorpe

*The view from the Gatehouse Tearooms*

**Distance:** 4 miles
**Terrain:** Footpaths and minor roads over undulating ground
**Map:** OS Landranger 133 North East Norfolk, Cromer & Wroxham (GR TG023353)

## How to get there

Gunthorpe is approximately 5 miles west of Holt. Turn south off the A148 for 2 miles following the signs to Gunthorpe. **Parking:** There is ample parking on the open ground alongside the parish church of St Mary.

# Drive and Stroll

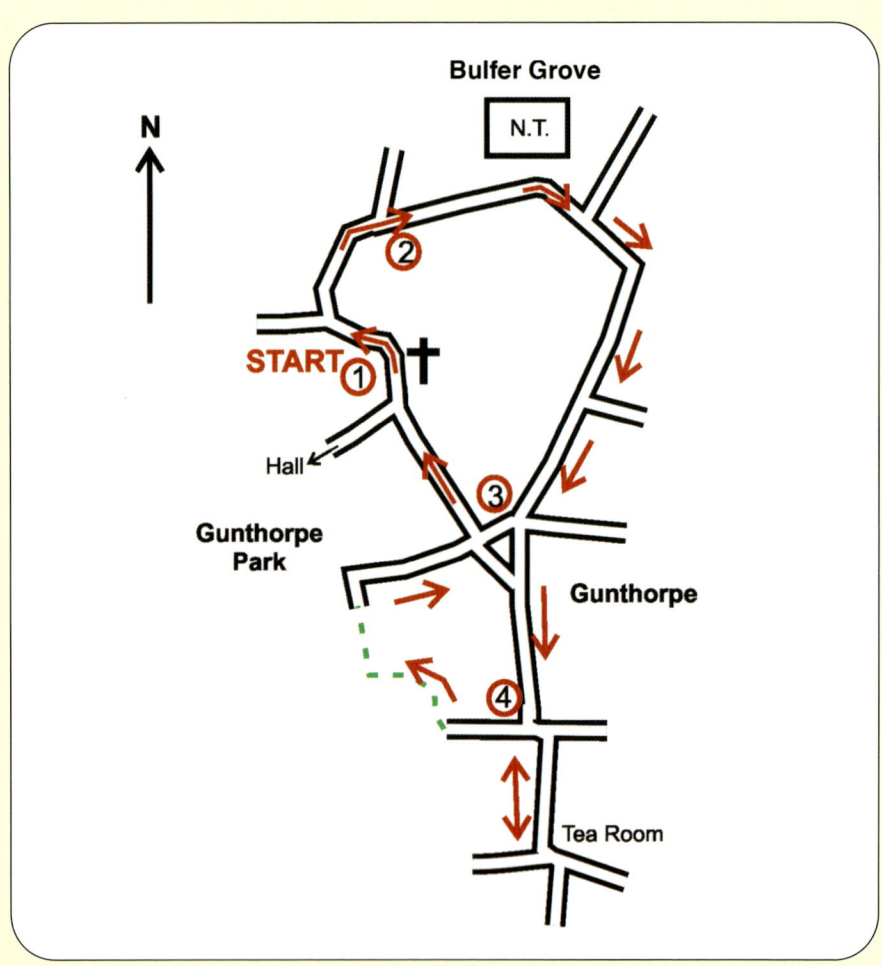

## Introduction
**This lovely stroll** offers almost continuous and delightful views of the parish church of Gunthorpe, as the route gently rises and falls around and beyond this peaceful village. The tracks pass through pretty countryside, whilst the narrow country lanes are almost devoid of traffic. Bulfer Grove, an area of woodland, can be explored along the way. Echoes of the once busy railway centre at the nearby village of Melton Constable are evident in the silent sentinel of the signal box, still standing at the Gatehouse tearooms.

# Around Gunthorpe

## Refreshments

The excellent **Gatehouse Tearooms** from which there are superb views of the countryside, are situated in the garden of a former Victorian railway crossing keeper's cottage, complete with original signal box by the gate! They offer light lunches, in addition to homemade cakes and tea, and are a treat not to be missed. They are open Thursday to Sunday 11 am to 5 pm from Easter through to the end of September. The tearooms are on the B1354 at the Gunthorpe and Swanton Novers crossroads, half a mile from Gunthorpe village. Telephone: 07919 937041.

The **John H Stacey pub** in nearby Melton Constable offers an alternative refreshment point. The town of Holt just beyond Letheringsett also has several cafés and restaurants.

## THE WALK

Turn right along the lane by the church.

*Across the road to the left is the old School House designed by Frederick Preedy of Worcester. Preedy also designed several of the church windows. The church of St Mary contains interesting Victorian stained glass windows, one of which commemorates Henry Spark, killed at Balaclava in 1834. His father, Canon Sparke, was the rector of the church.*

Continue along the lane as it bends right, then swing right along a wide green lane with trees on either side; this is **Bulfer Lane**. There are stunning views of the church to the right. Keep along the track as it bends, passing **Bulfer Grove Cottage** on the right. Just beyond this cottage turn right at the lane.

*A public bridleway leads into Bulfer Grove on the left. In the summer of 1919 these eight acres of woodland were given to the people of Britain by Sir Lawrence Jones, in thanks for the return of peace. His son was wounded and taken prisoner during the First World War. Now in the care of the National Trust, this little woodland makes a pleasant diversion from the walk.*

Continue on the lane for just over 300 yards. As it bends right, turn left along a wide track. After 50 yards, turn right by a post with the blue Norfolk County Council public bridleway sign. There is a hedge on the left and fields on the right as the wide footpath continues slightly uphill. At the path end turn right along the tarmac road to reach a

# Drive and Stroll

*St Mary's church near the start of the walk*

T-junction and the triangular village green.

(N.B. If you wish to shorten the walk, take the road to the right, signposted Bale, to return to the start of the walk.)

Using the signpost at the crossroads, take the road to **Swanton Novers**, (a bus timetable is attached to the post) passing cottages on the right, then the village hall on the left. Maintain direction passing the houses of The Stables Boundary Farm and The Barn, both of which have large garden ponds.

(N.B. If you wish to visit the **Gatehouse Tearooms** by foot and extend the walk, continue on the lane to the left, then turn right along the road, continuing for a little more

# 4 Around Gunthorpe

than ¼ mile to the Gatehouse. Retrace your steps to Boundary Farm.)

Beyond **Boundary Farm** turn right onto the wide track, marked 'Public Bridleway'. There is a modern windmill on the right and, shortly after, a view of Gunthorpe church, followed by modern farm buildings, also on the right. Follow the bridleway which initially has hedges on both sides, then a single hedge and stream on the right. At the end of the hedge, turn right following the stream to reach a fence. Turn left following the field edge towards a belt of trees. Before reaching the trees, however, turn right at a gap in the hedge with a bridge over the stream; continue through the gate and stile.

Go straight ahead on the green lane, **Heath Road**, running alongside several meadows which may contain cows. Follow the path turning left and passing through a large six-barred gate to reach a minor lane and turn right.
To the left at this lane is the tradesman's entrance to **Gunthorpe Hall**.

*The original part of Gunthorpe Hall was designed by Sir John Soane, architect of the Bank of England building in London. Today the hall is available to let for self-catering holiday; the Georgian and Victorian wings are now self-contained.*

Walk ahead on **Heath Lane** to arrive back at the village green. Turn left, signposted Bale, and walk uphill to return to the church and the start of the walk.

### Place of interest nearby

**Letheringsett Watermill** on the A148, one mile west of Holt, is one of Norfolk's last working mills. There are regular demonstrations, with the opportunity to buy flour and bread. The mill is open Monday to Saturday. Telephone: 01263 713153.

## Drive and Stroll

# 5 Paston Great Barn

*Striding out on the Paston Way*

**Distance:** 3½ miles
**Terrain:** Level footpaths and quiet lanes
**Map:** OS Landranger 133 North East Norfolk, Cromer & Wroxham (GR TG323343)

## How to get there

Paston village is on the B1159 coastal road, 2½ miles south of Mundesley town. **Parking:** In front of Paston Barn gates, just off the main road.

# 5 Paston Great Barn

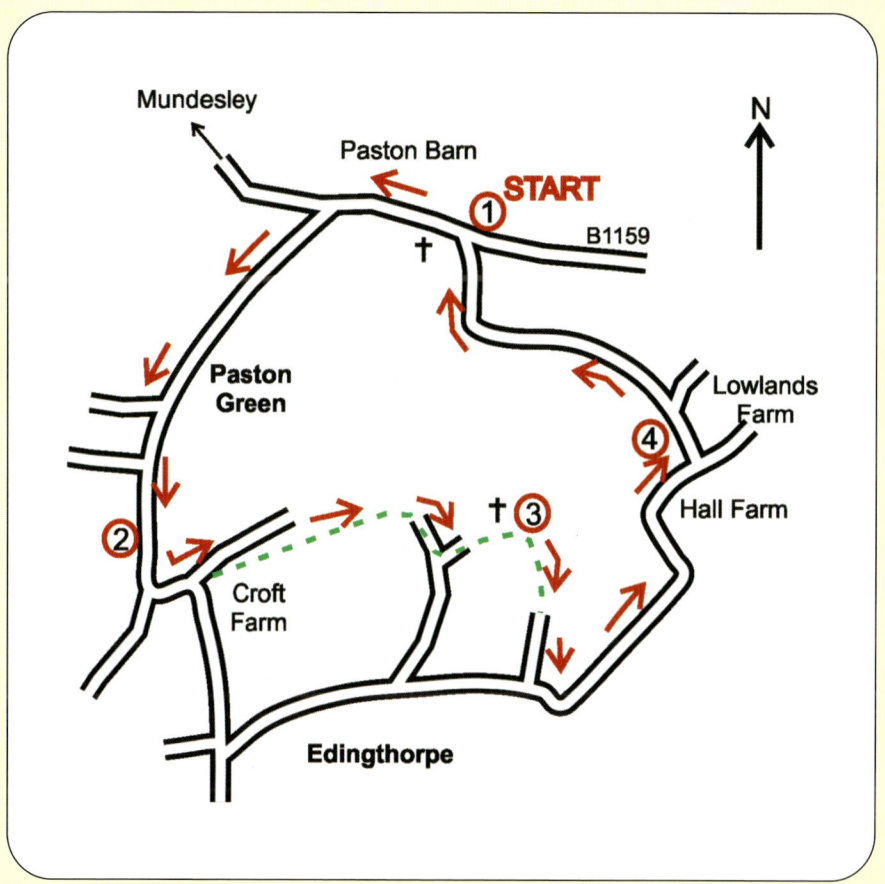

## Introduction
**This very enjoyable stroll** gives fine views of several medieval churches, emphasising the fact that Norfolk has more of these treasures than any other English county. Starting from Paston Great Barn, the route follows designated quiet lanes then crosses fields along the Paston Way. Edingthorpe, halfway through the walk, is an enchanting place to stop for a while. The circuit meanders from there through more quiet lanes, before passing Bacton gas terminal bringing you back to the 21st century and the start of the walk.

# Drive and Stroll

## Refreshments

The seaside town of Mundesley, 2½ miles away on the B1159, offers plenty of choice for refreshment. The **Manor Hotel**, the large edifice on Beach Road (telephone 01263 720309), and the **Royal Hotel** on Paston Road (telephone 01263 720096) both offer morning coffee, bar lunches and afternoon tea. They are open every day and each makes their visitors feel very welcome.

## THE WALK

*The Paston Great Barn is now home to the rare barbastelle bats of Batman fame, whose welfare currently precludes human visitors to the barn! A magnificent thatched building, this was built by Sir William Paston as a threshing barn, in the late 16th century.*

From the barn, view the outside of **St Margaret's** by going down the church drive and look for the wooden kissing gates on the right-hand side. Go through these and walk between the trees with **Paston Great Barn** on the right, to a further wooden kissing gate. Go ahead and at the minor road turn left. Continue on this stretch of road for almost ¾ mile.

*There is a lovely view here of Knapton church over to the right.*

Turn left, signposted 'Edingthorpe, Quiet Lanes'.

*The Quiet Lanes system is a project introduced in this area to make these little-used lanes better for walkers, cyclists and horse riders. The scheme has now been widened to include other parts of Norfolk.*

Continue on the lane as it bends to the right shortly after the turning. **Edingthorpe church**, where we are headed, can be seen in the distance. Just before reaching **Croft Farm** turn left at the yellow arrow sign marked N.C.C.P.F.P, onto a footpath.

*This path is part of the **Paston Way** long-distance path, its name derives from the Paston family. The Way takes in sixteen churches and sixteen villages and towns.*

Strike out ahead across the field, enjoying the superb views of **Edingthorpe church**. You can also see the gas terminal at this point. Cross the corner of the next field, then turn right along a clearly-defined path signposted 'Paston Way'. At the lane turn left and continue to **Edingthorpe church**.

# 5 Paston Great Barn

*Edingthorpe church*

# Drive and Stroll

*This lovely church was a childhood holiday haunt of the First World War poet, Siegfried Sassoon. The tranquil location and beautiful exterior lead to one of the most atmospheric and carefully tended interiors encountered on our walks.*

Upon leaving the church, continue on the lane, past the church, then turn right at the **Paston Way** sign. Go ahead passing through farm buildings to arrive at a country lane. Turn left and continue ahead following the winding lane.

*The distinctive red and white bands of Happisburgh lighthouse and the tall tower of the church form a scenic landscape at this point.*

After more than ½ mile take the turning to the left, signposted to **Bacton**, passing The Cherries, a house on the right. To the front of you is a fine view of Bacton gas terminal. Maintain direction, passing the terminal on the right.

*This terminal is one of five built over the last 35 years. It receives off-shore gas for use throughout the United Kingdom.*

Continue ahead, following the lane as it bends to arrive at the main road. Turn left and walk, with care, the short distance back to the start of the walk.

*St Margaret's church nearby contains several tombs of the Paston family, an important Norfolk family during the medieval and Tudor years. Their great legacy today lies with their wealth of correspondence, commonly referred to as 'The Paston Letters' that give a window onto life in medieval England. The tomb of Dame Katherine Paston, who died in 1628, is a sumptuous detailed memorial to a very 'chilled out' lady of means.*

## Place of interest nearby

**Stow Mill** is a little over a mile away. Take the B1159 towards Mundesley and the mill stands on the edge of the road. This brick tower mill was built as a flour mill between 1825 and 1827. It opens daily from 10 am to dusk all year round. Ices and take-away hot and cold drinks are available, with a place to sit outside if the weather allows. There is parking by the mill. Telephone: 01263 720298.

# Heydon and Salle

## 6 | Heydon and Salle

*The grand well on the village green in Heydon*

**Distance:** 3 miles
**Terrain:** Level footpaths and country lanes
**Map:** OS Landranger 133 North East Norfolk, Cromer & Wroxham (GR TG113275).

## How to get there

Heydon village is situated 12 miles north of Norwich, 2 miles off the B1149, Norwich to Holt road. It is signposted from the B1149. **Parking**: Turn left into the village car park which is located behind the Earle Arms public house.

# Drive and Stroll

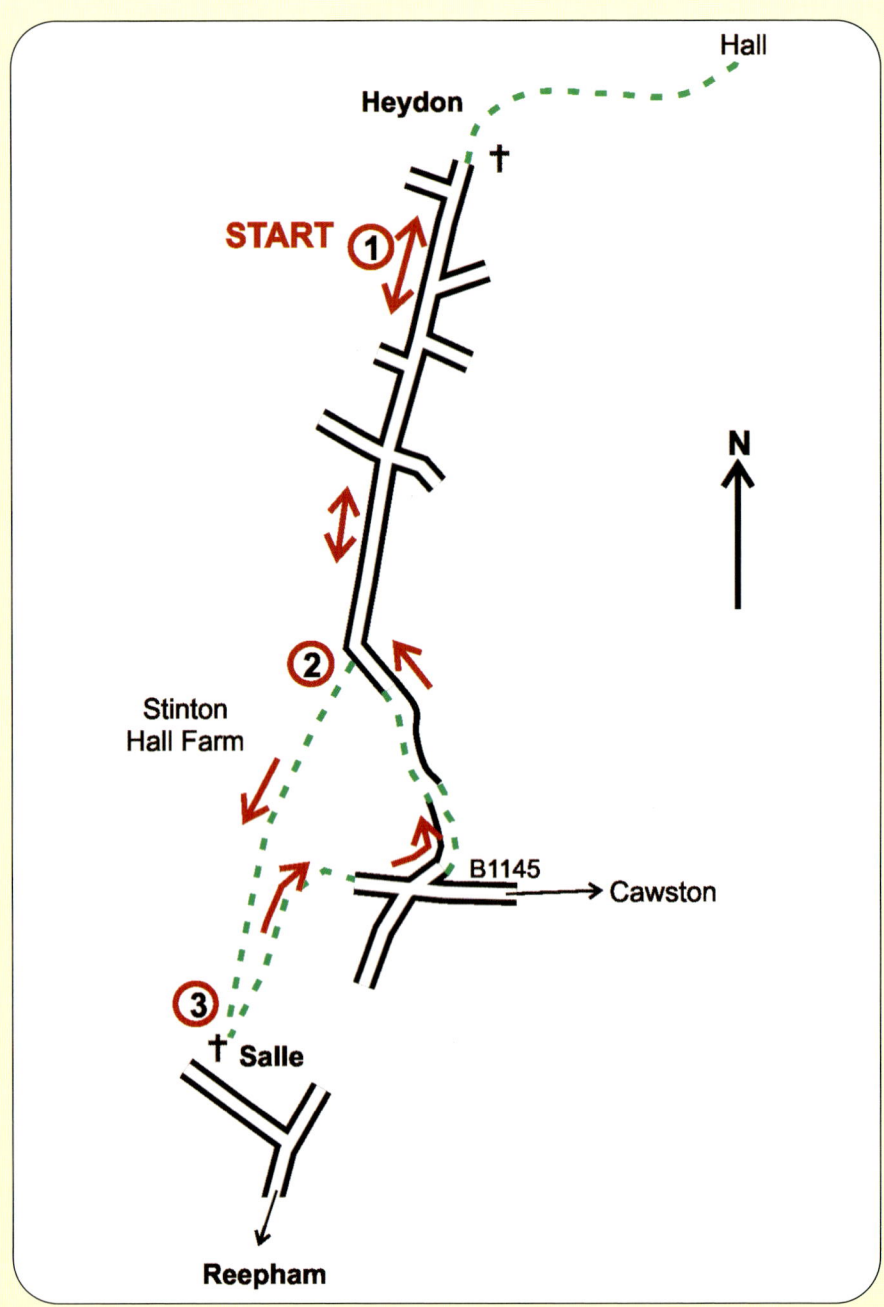

# 6 Heydon and Salle

## Introduction
**This easy to follow stroll** takes you from the delightful village of Heydon, one of less than a dozen villages in Britain which is still privately owned, to the tiny village of Salle with its superb 'wool' church. The walk is along pleasant country lanes and over open fields, offering splendid views of Salle church. Here you can rest awhile on the seat outside the church before returning, passing the magnificent Salle Estate, to rejoin the country lane that takes you back to the start of the walk.

## Refreshments
**Heydon Village Tea Room and Shop** is a very special tea room, reflecting its unique surroundings. You can sit outside facing the village green, where there is a well, built to commemorate the Jubilee of Queen Victoria in 1887; or you can relax within its traditional walls. The tea room serves light lunches, homemade cakes and cream teas, and you are assured of a warm welcome. Telephone 01263 587719.

## THE WALK

From the car park we recommend that you turn left and go through the park gates to take a peek at Heydon Hall, and view the church.

*The wall paintings inside the church were hidden from view until 1970, when the wall was cleaned. The hall, which is not open to the public, was built in 1582. Extensive restoration during the 1970s led to the demolition of many 19th-century additions, and the hall has now been returned to its Elizabethan proportions. Visitors are welcome to walk in the grounds of the park.*

Retrace your steps and continue ahead to the crossroads, passing pretty cottages and the large village green.

*There has been no new building in the village since the construction of the well and, unsurprisingly, Heydon has been much in demand for the filming of period productions. Some of the best known of these are:* The Go-Between, Vanity Fair, Love on the Branch Line *and* Moonstone.

At the crossroads go straight over, signposted 'Salle 1½ miles' and walk ahead. This is a lovely country lane, time seems to have stood still here as well!

Just beyond the 'road bends' sign, swing right across the wooden

33

# Drive and Stroll

Salle's village sign, made to commemorate Queen Elizabeth II's coronation

# 6 | Heydon and Salle

footbridge, over a ditch and into the field. There is a yellow circular footpath sign here. Continue along the well-defined footpath aiming for **Salle church,** seen in the distance. Go ahead to cross the footbridge over the stream. Maintain direction across the next field and go through the gap in the hedge to reach the church. The tower of St Agnes church, Cawston, is visible to the right in the distance.

*Go through a gap in the churchyard wall to visit Salle church and its interior.*

*This superb church was built during the 15th century. It owes much of its construction to the wealth derived from sheep; from their wool and the families who accumulated their wealth in its trade, hence the term 'wool church'. There is much of interest. Take note especially of the fantastic carvings on the fine oak stalls. An excellent guide can be found inside at a cost of 20p!*

Exit via the lych-gate, to find a well-placed bench near the village sign if you wish to take a break.

*The sign was made by Harry Carter to commemorate the coronation of Queen Elizabeth II.*

To continue your walk, retrace your steps out of the churchyard via the gap in the wall; going back across the first field; turn right at the finger-post and continue ahead to reach the lane. Turn left.

Continue on the lane, passing **Manor Farm** on the right. Just beyond this, where the lane forks, take the left-hand fork, signposted to Heydon and Guestwick. Walk ahead on the lane, crossing an attractive bridge. Maintain direction to reach the section of the lane walked earlier and continue ahead, retracing your steps on this final part of the walk to arrive back in **Heydon** village.

## Place of interest nearby

**Mannington Hall Gardens** have a superb rose collection; the garden is listed as Grade II for English Heritage. It is open May to September and the surrounding parkland is open all year round. The hall itself is not open to members of the public. Take the B1149 to the village of Saxthorpe, then follow the brown tourist signs. The gardens are just beyond Saxthorpe on a minor road. Telephone 01263 584175.

## Drive and Stroll

# 7 Congham

*Congham Hall is the perfect spot to enjoy some refreshment after your walk*

**Distance:** 2½ miles
**Terrain:** Level footpaths and short sections of country lanes
**Map:** OS Explorer 23 Norfolk Coast West, King's Lynn & Hunstanton (GR TF713238).

### How to get there

Congham village is located off the A148, on a minor road, 6 miles north-east of King's Lynn. **Parking:** In the lay-by between Congham Hall and the cricket ground, on the road running from the A148 through Congham to Great Massingham.

# 7 Congham

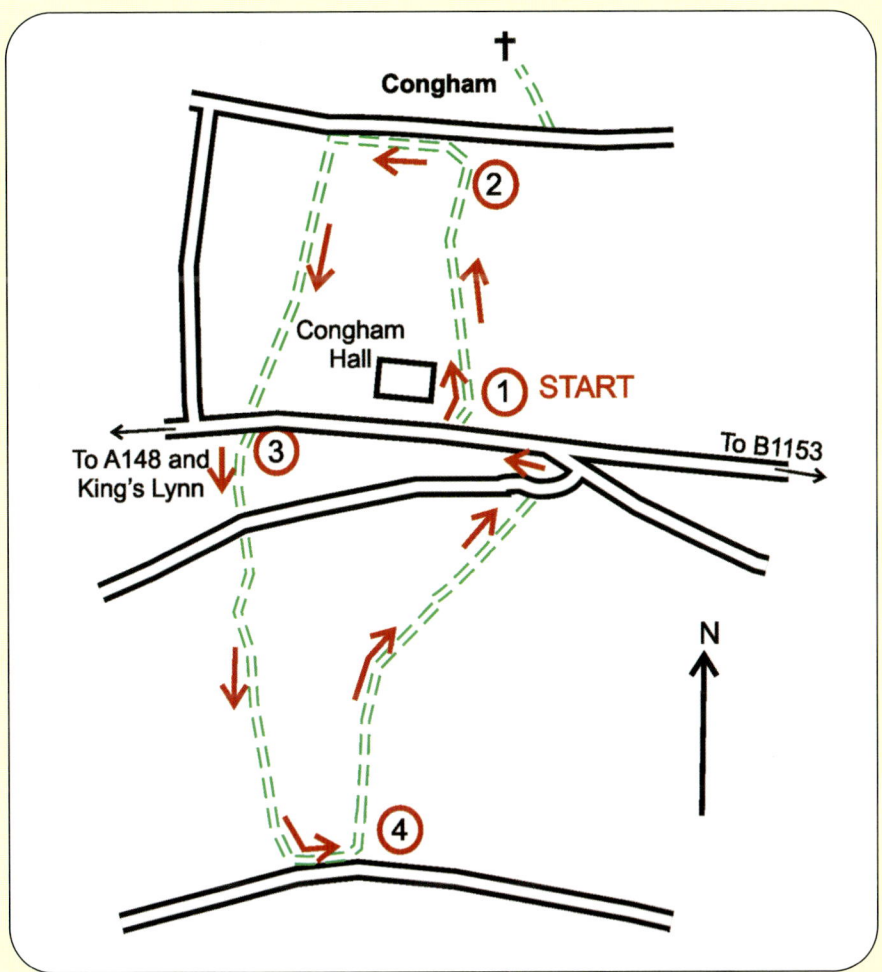

## Introduction
**Congham, perhaps, surprisingly**, is the venue for a world championship event – snail racing! Every year at Congham cricket field, where the walk begins, crowds gather to watch this spectacle. This curcuit, which is almost all on footpaths, passes close to Congham Hall, continues to the parish church of Congham, and journeys through fields, before arriving back at the start. Whether you go at speed or snail's pace, ensure you take time out for a very English cream tea at Congham Hall.

# Drive and Stroll

## Refreshments

A description of **Congham Hall Hotel** must be full of superlatives, all of which are justified. This elegant Georgian manor is set amongst beautiful parkland. Within its grounds there is a wonderful herb garden, which is free to visit. The terrace, where in summer you can partake of afternoon tea, overlooks the immaculate lawns and spreading trees. The service provided is superb and the cakes delicious! Visit this exceptional hotel for a memorable cup of tea! Telephone: 01485 600250.

## THE WALK

Walk from the car to the entrance of the cricket ground, going around the white five-bar gate. Continue ahead, passing the thatched archetypal cricket pavilion, to the footpath sign at the end of the field.

*This ground is the battle site of the Snail Championship. Up to 300 snails enter, taking part in a series of heats to reach the final.*

Follow the diagonal green path from the cricket ground to reach a footbridge and a County Council yellow waymark sign. Continue along the short narrow path to the next post with the yellow sign. The herb garden at **Congham Hall** can be seen on the left, as you walk away from the cricket ground.

Turn right into a well-maintained paddock, then exit from its top left-hand corner. Continue straight ahead to reach a further post and yellow waymark sign. Turn right then left and follow the path with a hedge to the right to arrive at a narrow country lane.

Turn right here to visit **Congham church**, visible through the trees.

*St Andrew's church is carefully tucked away, but worth a visit; the contact details for the key-holder are provided. The church is reached, through the gated entrance, by a narrow pedestrian pathway, with an impressive arcade of mature trees. The pathway is long and the church, set a considerable way back from the lane, sits in splendid isolation surrounded by trees.*

Retrace your steps and return to the lane. Turn right, passing the red telephone box and post box seen earlier. Continue ahead, passing stone cottages on the right, and then the **Anvil public house**, where you could take a break. Look for the footpath sign on the left,

# 7 Congham

opposite a bungalow on the right, **The Birches**, and just past a side road and the Anvil public house. Turn left at the footpath sign into the field, following the well-marked path towards some trees.

*The ditch running alongside is a haven for wild flowers and rabbits.*

The path becomes a grassy one leading to another post and yellow waymark sign. Continue along the field edge to reach a further sign and a plank bridge. Cross the bridge and walk ahead on the short woodland path to a modern wooden gate. Go through the gate into the meadow, heading for the tree between the two modern houses straight ahead. Pass the tree and walk to the stile seen in the narrow passage between the houses. Climb the stile and walk the short path to reach the road ahead. Turn right, then cross the road before the **Three Horseshoes public house**, to **Jasmine Cottage**.

*The Three Horseshoes offers another chance for more refreshment!*

Continue straight ahead, ignoring the tarmac lane, and follow the broad grassy path to reach a low stile. Cross over the stile and turn right, passing a pair of cottages,

*Bullrushes can be seen in the dykes along the route*

onto a tarmac lane, but almost immediately go left at the kissing gate and footpath sign.

Follow the path to the next kissing gate and go through into a field with poles and power lines. Follow the poles and then the emerging hedge on the right through the field to reach a road and turn left along it. Continue past the yellow house.

Turn left off the road, where the farm buildings end, and follow the main farmyard track to reach a large pink-coloured shed on the right. Turn right immediately after

*39*

# Drive and Stroll

the shed to cross the line of the dyke, and then immediately left. Continue ahead with the dyke now on the left.

*There are bullrushes in these dykes and a good view of Grimston church ahead.*

Turn left into the next field and follow the field edge to the footpath sign, and thence the road. Turn and, soon after, bear left onto **Lynn Road**, by some pretty cottages.

The entrance to the cricket field and the start of the walk is now visible. Continue along the road to visit **Congham Hall Hotel** and the herb garden.

*The Herb Garden is reached from the drive to the hotel and is signposted. It is open for visitors and plant sales, from 2 pm to 4 pm. There are over 700 varieties in the kitchen garden and it is well worth a visit.*

### Place of interest nearby

**Castle Rising castle ruins** are an impressive sight, with a Norman keep and a formidable bank surrounding the one-time moat. This is an English Heritage site and is open daily from April to October. To visit, return to the A148 and turn left to the Knight's Hill roundabout. Turn right onto the A149 heading for Sandringham and Hunstanton. The castle can be found on the left in just over a mile.

# 8 | Whissonsett

*The 16th-century barn near Godwick*

**Distance:** 3 miles
**Terrain:** Level footpaths, uphill climb through fields on the return
**Map:** OS Landranger 132 North West Norfolk, King's Lynn & Fakenham (GR TF918233).

## How to get there

Whissonsett lies on a minor road 2½ miles east of the A1065, Swaffham to Fakenham road, and 6½ miles south-west of Fakenham. **Parking:** In the High Street, outside the parish church of St Mary.

# Drive and Stroll

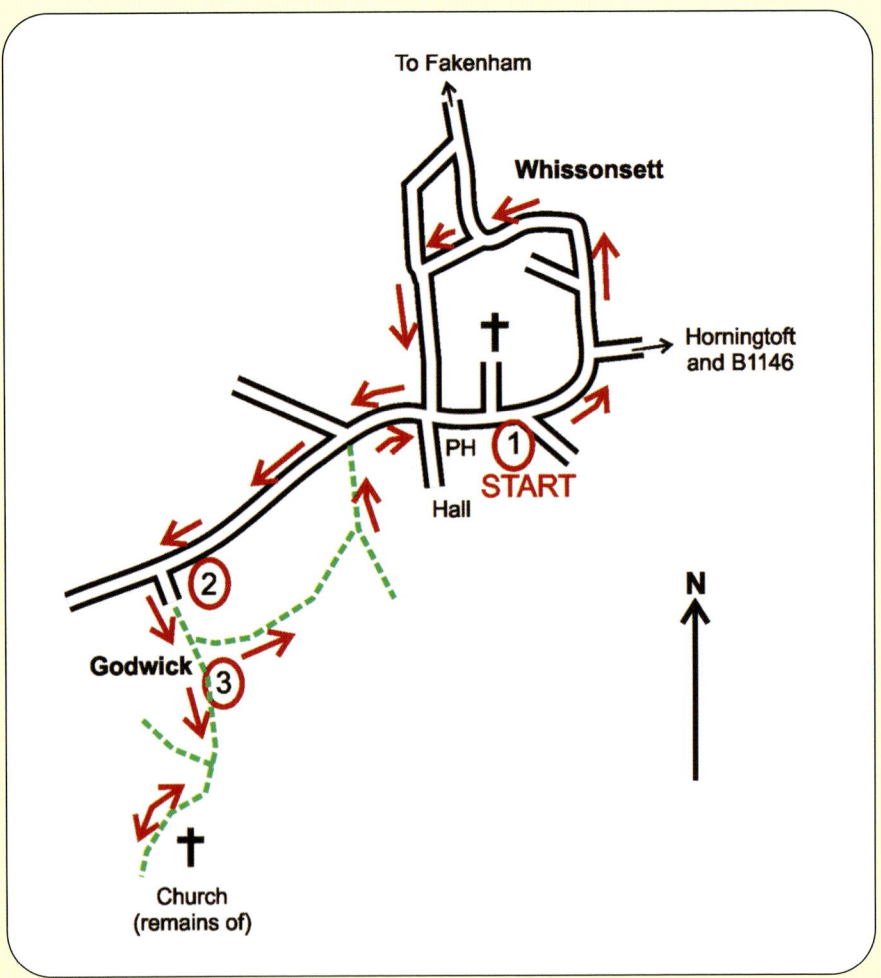

## Introduction
**This fascinating walk** begins at the church of St Mary in the peaceful village of Whissonsett, home of two brothers who became heroes in the Second World War. The route explores the pretty village before passing farmland with wide-open views. It then travels to a deserted medieval village, one of the best examples in the country, and returns via a working farm and several fields uphill, before reaching a country lane leading back to the start.

# 8 Whissonsett

## Refreshments

There is no longer a public house in Whissonsett but the excellent **Brisley Bell** is little more than 2 miles east of Whissonsett along minor roads. Continue through Brisley, passing the parish church, and the Bell can be found on the left of the large green. It is open every day except Monday. This is a very friendly hostelry and a splendid place for refreshments. Telephone: 01362 668686.

## THE WALK

*The open area of grass in front of the church at the start of this walk is the Camping Land, the name deriving from a very rough game called Camp where injuries were common. Do visit the mainly 14th-century church which houses, amongst other treasures, an Anglo-Saxon cross, dug up in the churchyard in 1902.*

On leaving the churchyard, turn left along the **High Street**, passing the colourful and informative village sign on the left.

*The two military figures in the centre are the brothers Lieutenant Colonel Derek Seagrim, holder of the Victoria Cross, and Major Hugh Seagrim, holder of the George Cross. They were two of the sons of a former rector of Whissonsett and are, as yet, the only brothers ever to be awarded the two highest bravery awards. Their poignant stories are too lengthy to record here, but they are well documented and worth time researching. Their monument can be seen near the entrance to the church. Their brother Jack said of their childhood in Whissonsett, 'We were as poor as church mice but had a wonderful life in the village; it was totally classless'.*

Go ahead past the post office.

*This is one of the oldest buildings in the village. It has been a post office since 1917 and, most remarkably, since then has had only three postmasters and mistresses.*

Turn left into **New Road** – look out for the miniature stocks! Continue ahead, passing what was once the King's Head public house and turn left into **Springwell Road**, where the ancient spring can still be seen. At the next junction turn left into **London Road**.

*On the right is a Victorian letterbox and nearby is the site of the first Whissonsett post office.*

Walk ahead for 200 yards to arrive back at the **High Street**. Turn right

# Drive and Stroll

opposite what used to be the Swan public house and continue along the road taking the left-hand fork at **Mill Lane**, signposted 'Tittleshall and Litcham', passing **Rodwell Farm** on the left.

*There are fine agricultural views all around as you walk down the lane. This area is working farmland and the crops grown here include mint, parsley and blackcurrants, some of which are harvested for the Ribena brand.*

 ②

Continue along the lane to reach a large sign on the right for Godwick Farms and Suffolk Sheep and Godwick Historic Nature Walk. Turn left just beyond the sign, walking along a farm drive. On the left in the autumn we saw a large flock of turkeys in the field. Continue, passing **Godwick Hall Farm** on the right. The ruins of Godwick church can be seen in the distance and presently you arrive at the map and information boards relating to the deserted village of **Godwick**. Turn right at the footpath sign, just after the boards, and walk across the grassy meadow to visit the site.

Until the 15th century, Godwick was a small but stable village, however, a survey made in 1508 showed that many properties were empty and by 1595 Godwick was virtually

All that remains of Godwick church

deserted. One of the reasons for its decline was the loss of work, as ploughed land was turned into pasture for sheep. There are information boards around the site, which is considered a fine example of a deserted medieval village and for which the owner of the land generously allows free access. Note the rather spectacular late 16th-century barn built in the field nearby.

 ③

Return to the farm drive and go through the farm buildings opposite

# 8 Whissonsett

to arrive at the field edge. (We checked with the farmer who was happy for us to go between the buildings but please remember this is a working farm and take care to avoid any machinery.) Maintain direction across the field to the large gap in the hedge visible on the rise. Continue across the next field, aiming to the right of the middle telegraph post, to reach the next hedge gap where there is a post and yellow arrow sign clearly visible ahead. Go through to the next field and turn immediately left along the field for about 200 yards. Turn right, keeping to the field edge, to the next Norfolk County Council marker sign on the left. Turn left through the gap into a further field. Follow the very well-defined path going diagonally across the fields to reach a green lane. Turn left along the path to arrive at a minor road. Turn right to return to the village and the start of the walk.

## Place of interest nearby

**Gressenhall Rural Life Museum** is 4 miles south of Whissonsett on the B1156. This highly acclaimed and interesting museum, housed in the former Union Workhouse, is open daily from 10 am. Telephone the 24-hour information line 01362 869263, or ring 01362 860563.

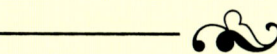

# Drive and Stroll

# 9 Horsey

*The path through the dunes*

**Distance:** 5 miles
**Terrain**: Good paths, flat except for a climb through the sand dunes to the beach. Children should be supervised beside the stretches of open water.
**Map**: OS Outdoor Leisure 40; The Broads (GR TQ457224).

## How to get there

Horsey is on the B1159, 4 miles south of Sea Palling and 3 miles north of Martham. **Parking:** National Trust pay & display car park, Horsey Windpump.

# 9 Horsey

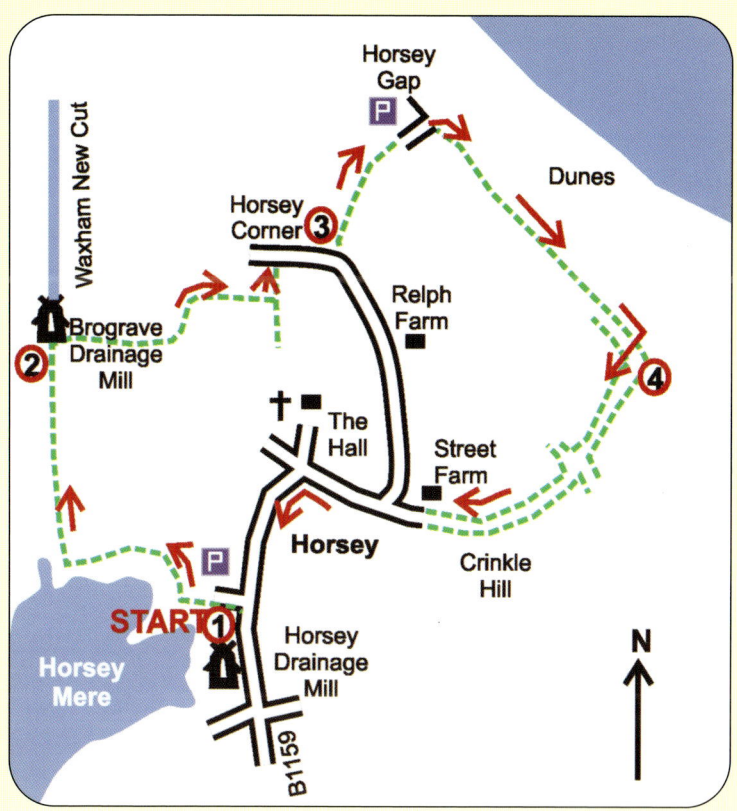

## Introduction
**Horsey is one of the few** places where the coast and broads can be walked within a few hundred yards of each other. This lovely walk passes Horsey Mere, a picturesque expanse of water, crossing fields and dykes to a golden beach filled with sand dunes. It returns via the well-known landmark of Horsey Windpump, a favourite subject for local artists.

## Refreshments
The charming **Poppylands Restaurant** is open daily from 10 am during the summer season and at weekends from November to Easter. In addition to the lunches and afternoons teas which are served daily, there is an all-day breakfast available on Saturday and a carvery at Sunday lunchtime.

# Drive and Stroll

## THE WALK

From the car park, walk to the steps and footpath sign, then turn right along the towpath. Follow the path and boardwalk until it reaches a gate.

*To the left are wonderful views of Horsey mere, and sometimes there is livestock in the fields. The mere is an important winter habitat for wildfowl.*

Go through the gate and cross the field diagonally left to a further gate, go through this and continue along the path and boardwalk to reach **the Cut**.

*The surrounding area, which has often been subject to flooding, some of it severe, is part of the Horsey Estate, owned by the National Trust and, as the walk demonstrates, it is very peaceful and tranquil.*

Continue alongside the water's edge to the ruined windpump ahead and the end of the path.

*The ruined windpump is Brograve Mill, much photographed by holidaymakers. There is ongoing restoration of windmills and windpumps previously left to the elements; many have been capped and some have acquired new sails.*

Turn right, climb the stile and walk on the field edge to the houses ahead. Climb the stile at the end of the path to reach a lane. Turn left along the lane and walk to the main road. Turn right along this road walking with care as it can be very busy at times.

At the sharp bend turn left down the gravel track, taking you back into the **Horsey Estate**, to reach a small car parking area and **Horsey Warren**. There is a choice of route here; you can turn right going through the kissing gate and along the path by the dunes or, if you prefer, you can continue ahead through the gap to reach the sea and turn right to walk along the beach.

*This is a wide golden beach of sand, where occasionally you can see a seal bobbing off the shoreline. They are to be found on the beach at certain times of the year at Winterton-on-Sea, the next parish eastward.*

Turn right at the next concrete gap onto a wide fenced track. If you

# 9 Horsey

choose the beach walk, then you will need to turn right, away from the beach, climbing the short sand hill, the track is then directly ahead of you.

Continue on this track to arrive at a road, passing the Nelson Head public house. Turn right onto the road, then turn left along it, following it back to the car park. This road is busy and must be walked with care, using the grass verge as much as possible.

All Saints church, with its round tower and long, low thatched nave and chancel speak of a church that has remained unchanged for centuries. It is on the road leading back to the car park and is well worth a visit.

Turn left as you enter the car park to visit the wind pump.

Horsey windpump is featured on many postcards of this area. Now

*The atmospheric ruin that was once Brograve Mill*

owned by the National Trust, the current building dates from 1912 but there has been a mill here for much longer. It is open from March to October at weekends and daily during the high season.

## Place of interest nearby

**Waxham Great Barn** is the longest barn in the county, surpassing the Paston Great Barn seen on another walk, and is in an equally lovely setting. There is ample car parking for visiting this beautiful Tudor barn and its exhibition. The unspoilt beach of Waxham is very close, and the parish church in the nearby field is well worth a visit. Refreshments are available in the tea lounge. The Barn is open April to October. Telephone: 01692 598824.

## Drive and Stroll

# 10 Neatishead

*The big expanse that is Barton Broad*

**Distance:** 2¾ miles
**Terrain:** Flat footpaths, country lanes and board walk
**Map:** OS Explorer OL40 The Broads (GR TG351207)

### How to get there

Neatishead village is 3 miles north-east of Wroxham, signposted off the A1151. In Neatishead village turn right along the Irstead road, at Ye Olde Saddlery. After half a mile turn right, signposted 'Boardwalk', then after 150 yards turn left into the specially appointed car park. **Parking**: In the car park, where there is also a toilet block.

# 10 Neatishead

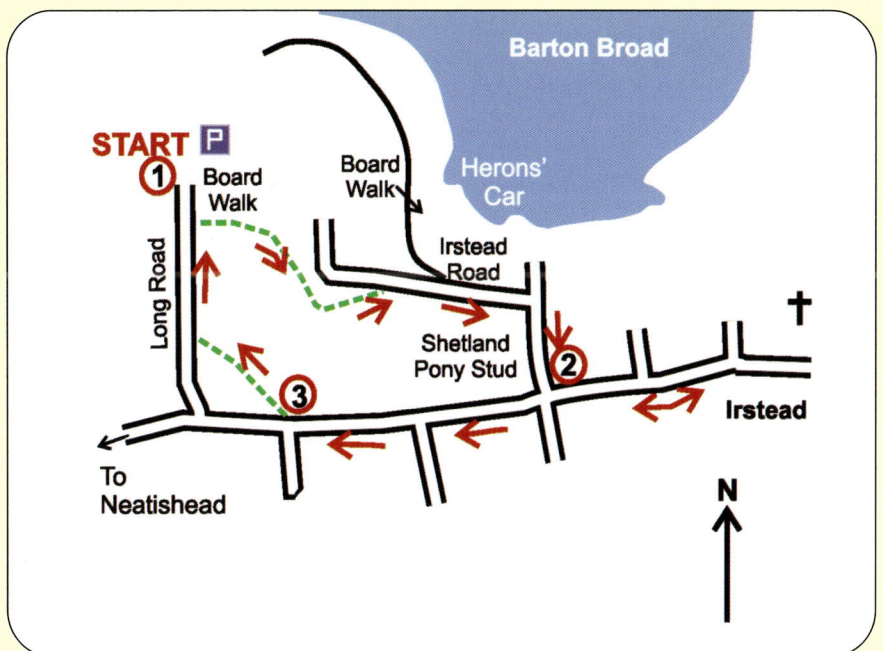

## Introduction
**This delightful stroll** along lanes and footpaths is in the heart of Norfolk's beautiful Broadland. Starting near the pretty village of Neatishead, the walk takes you to a very special ½-mile long boardwalk designed especially with disabled visitors in mind. This easily accessible boardwalk leads to a viewing platform overlooking Barton Broad where the views are quite simply stunning. The stroll continues to the pretty thatched church at Irstead, looks to the river nearby, then returns to the start via lanes and footpaths.

## Refreshments
**Ye Olde Saddlery** is a very pleasant restaurant open daily during the summer season. It serves meals from 12 noon to 2.30 pm and again from 6 pm to 8.30 pm. It uses locally sourced fish, meat and vegetables wherever possible. It has a popular Sunday carvery and specialises in gluten-free dishes. The bar opens all day for morning coffee or afternoon tea. Telephone: 01692 630866.

The **White Horse Inn** on the opposite side of the road is an equally welcoming public house. Food is served in a separate dining area and the inn is open daily. Telephone: 01692 630828.

# Drive and Stroll

## THE WALK

Exit the car park at the large circular information panel, opposite the signpost 'Boardwalk'. Follow the specially constructed path as it turns to arrive at a tarmac lane and another boardwalk sign. (N.B. This path does not appear on the OS map.) Continue ahead along the lane until a set of three marked posts appears on the left; this is the entrance to the boardwalk itself. It is possible to go in either direction but this walk describes it as turning left at this point.

*The boardwalk was opened in 2004 following two years of construction. It is built above ground level, similar to a pontoon and leads through swampy ground and trees of all kinds within a National Nature Reserve. There are information boards at points all along the boardwalk, including one describing its construction. There are also braille tablets at intervals on the walk.*

Continue on the boardwalk, then take the next leftward option, this leads to the viewing platform and additional information boards.

*Barton Broad is the second largest of the Norfolk Broads and the platform gives outstanding views, normally only available from the water. In the years between 1760-1780, Admiral Nelson spent a lot of time here visiting relatives. The Broads were formed during medieval times from digging peat for fuel. The 20th century saw a marked deterioration in the quality of the banks and the water and, in 1995, the Broads Authority began a major restoration project to return it to a healthy state. The information boards catalogue its progress.*

Returning from the platform, turn left to continue, ignoring the path signed 'car-park only' and turn right to complete the boardwalk. Return to the lane and turn left passing a car park for disabled visitors to the boardwalk and continue ahead to reach a crossroads and 'Give way' sign.

Turn right and walk ahead to arrive at the **parish church of Irstead**.

*The thatched church has been described as a 'gem of a small church' and 'not to be missed' and this is indeed the case. The thatch is of local reed and sedge with traditional decoration. St Michael's is open during daylight hours and worthy of a visit.*

Continue the few yards past the church to reach **Irstead Staithe** and the **River Ant**.

# 10            Neatishead

*This is a very pretty spot with convenient benches for a break and contemplation of the river scene.*

Leave the staithe and return by the lane to the crossroads reached earlier.

*Note the oak tree with its iron fencing at the end of the driveway of the Old Hall, by the crossroads. This was planted in 1953 to celebrate the Coronation of Queen Elizabeth II.*

At the crossroads continue straight ahead, signposted 'Three Hammer Common'. Pass two turns to the left to **Irstead Street**, and after the second of these go right at the footpath sign, climbing the bank into the field.

Part of the boardwalk that leads through the reserve

Follow the clearly marked path as it goes diagonally across the field to arrive at a country lane (there is no footpath sign here), then turn right along the lane. Continue ahead to arrive back at the car park on the right.

## Place of interest nearby

**Neatishead RAF Radar Museum** is an unusual museum which has won several awards since its inception. It traces the history of Air Defence Radar. The displays and equipment shown are all authentic and you can wander as you wish, or join a guided tour. The museum is a little over 2 miles from Neatishead using the minor roads, or you can return to the A1151, turn left and the museum is signposted off the main road on the left. It is open on the second Saturday of the month all year, with additional opening hours from April to October. Telephone: 01692 631485.

# Drive and Stroll

## 11 Lyng and Elsing

*The moated manor house passed on the way*

**Distance:** 4 miles
**Terrain:** Slightly undulating footpaths and lanes
**Map**: OS Landranger 133 North East Norfolk, Cromer & Wroxham (GR TG069178).

### How to get there

Lyng is situated on a minor road off the A1067, 4 miles south-west of Reepham, 10 miles north-west of Norwich. **Parking:** In the small car park opposite the Fox & Hounds public house in Lyng.

# 11 Lyng and Elsing

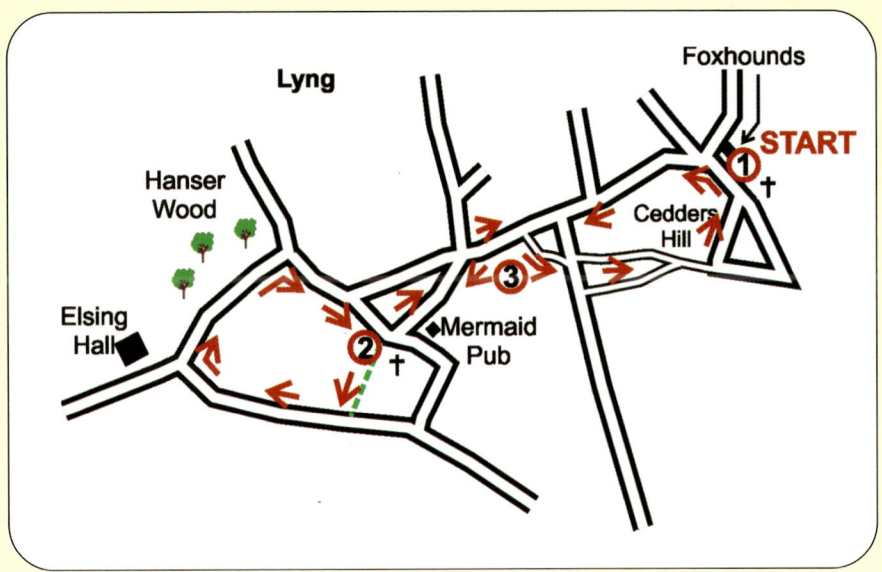

## Introduction
**This pleasant walk** incorporates two lovely villages, using a mixture of footpaths and quiet country lanes, and visits two interesting churches. In spring and summer wild flowers proliferate along the lane edges as the stroll undulates through a variety of countryside.

## Refreshments
The **Fox and Hounds** is full of character, with a friendly atmosphere. It is a free house serving excellent food daily. Telephone: 01603 872316.

## THE WALK

Turn left out of the car park and continue along **The Street**. After a short distance turn left again into **Heath Road**, signposted 'Elsing 1 mile'. Continue ahead.

This lane is very peaceful and pretty with woodland to both sides. It is reminiscent of how we imagine the quiet country lanes of long ago.

At the next T-junction turn left into **Church Road**, signposted 'Bylaugh' and continue to the T-junction. Turn left towards the **Mermaid Inn** and the parish church of St Mary the Virgin.

55

# Drive and Stroll

*This Decorated church built in the 14th century is unusual in Norfolk in that it was built in one go, early in the century and suffered little change. It was built by Sir Hugh Hastings and it remained as he intended whilst the fashionable updates of the 15th century commonly found, passed it by. There is a memorial brass to Sir Hugh, of European importance, inside the church. The font canopy is also very attractive. More information can be found inside.*

*There is a wonderful view of the church from the gardens of the welcoming Mermaid Inn should you decide on a refreshment stop. A public house has been on this site for centuries, variously called the Mermaid, Meremaid and Moormade!*

After visiting the church turn left along the lane, then turn left after a few yards at the footpath sign. Walk the footpath between the fields to reach a minor road and turn right along it.

If you wish to view **Elsing Hall**, or include your visit within the walk, turn left at this point and walk down the drive to the hall. Otherwise turn right along the lane and continue ahead passing **Harnser Wood** on the left.

*The Woodland Trust, a charity that aims to conserve and re-establish the United Kingdom's woodland, created Harnser Wood. Harnser is the Norfolk term for the heron.*

Walk along the lane to the village sign and turn right to the **Mermaid Inn**.

*In 1978 members of Elsing Women's Institute raised £250 to pay for the village sign. It depicts a Danish chieftain, Elesa, and his wolfhound, and the watermill; the sign was made by Harry Carter, who was renowned for his work on village signs.*

Retrace your steps taken earlier in the walk from the public house to the crossroads and turn right into **Heath Road,** passing the attractive chapel on the left.

Look for the yellow marker sign in the woodland on the right and turn onto the well defined path through the woods. At the path end turn left at the public footpath finger-post sign and continue ahead to reach a minor lane. The views here of the rolling countryside are lovely. Cross straight over the lane taking the footpath almost opposite. Maintain direction onto a sandy path that veers right and then slightly uphill to reach a country lane.

# 11 Lyng and Elsing

Cadders Hill, to the left, is home to the Norwich Vikings who have organised moto-cross events here since 1936.

Turn left onto the lane, continue ahead to the junction with **The Street** and turn right towards the **parish church of Lyng** and the start of the walk.

The church of St Margaret is on the loke (a local word for a small dead end lane) around the corner from the Fox & Hounds public house. One unusual feature inside the church is the altar cloth in a glass case on the west wall. It is made from three 15th-century vestments of red, blue and orange velvet. On the advice of embroidery experts from Hampton Court in 1983, funds were made available for its restoration. This was beautifully completed by the restorer Wendy Toulson, and the altar cloth was returned to the church in 1985.

*The colourful village sign in Elsing*

### Place of interest nearby

**Elsing Hall** is a moated manor house built in the 15th century by the Hastings family. It was extensively restored by Thomas Jackyll in 1852. The hall is open to the public on Sunday, June to October from 2 pm to 6 pm. There are over 500 varieties of roses planted by the current owner. Telephone: 01362 637224.

## Drive and Stroll

# 12 Walpole St Peter and Walpole St Andrew

*In Walpole Water Gardens*

**Distance:** 4½ miles
**Terrain:** Flat lanes and footpaths
**Map**: OS Landranger 131 Boston & Spalding (GR TF503168)

### How to get there

Walpole St Peter is 2 miles west of King's Lynn and lies between the trunk roads of the A17, 4 miles to the north, and the A47, 2½ miles to the south. Follow the brown church signs in the village. **Parking**: On Church Road beside St Peter's church.

# 12 Walpole St Peter and Walpole St Andrew

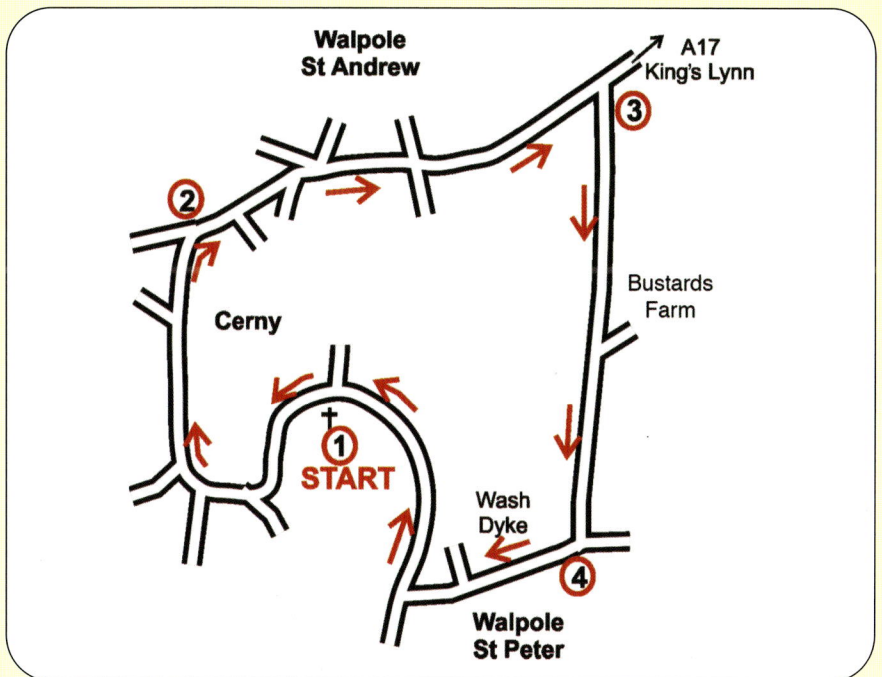

## Introduction
**The fens and marshes** of West Norfolk offer a walk with a difference; the flat landscape and vast skies can be viewed at their very best here. There is an eerie atmosphere sometimes, no surprise really as this is the land of the legendary giant Tom Hickathrift and the lost treasure of King John. This walk takes you via two magnificent churches into that landscape, returning by way of Walpole Water Gardens where a visit is an absolute must!

## Refreshments
The **Walpole Water Gardens** advertises itself as 'probably the best value tea room in East Anglia'. It certainly must rank as one of the most unusual! The totally unexpected feel of a tropical oasis in this otherwise flat landscape gives it an exotic charm. Beautiful black swans, hungry Koi carp and curious cats are all there to greet the visitor, as well as the owner, Peter Cousins. Peter's paintings feature in the gallery next to the tea room, where hot and cold drinks and snacks are available. The gardens are free to enter and open all year round, closing only on Christmas Day. You are assured of a warm welcome and a good cup of tea! Telephone: 07718 745935.

# Drive and Stroll

## THE WALK

*Start by first exploring the church, known as the 'Queen of the Marshlands'. It was built with the profits made from sheep, the land being particularly suitable for their rearing. There is much of interest inside whilst an unusual feature outside is the 'bolt hole', a passageway with a marvellous vaulted roof created under the high altar.*

*The little stone figure on the wall is said to be of the giant Tom Hickathrift, although he is actually buried at Tilney All Saints. Tom became a hero long ago for ridding the area of a dreadful ogre! This wonderful church is believed by many to be one of the finest in England, it is also one of the most visited.*

Leave the churchyard at **Church Road** and turn left. Continue to the T-junction and turn right into **Walnut Road**, following this as it bends right where it becomes **Police Road**. Maintain direction passing an apple orchard and the town cemetery on the right.

*The Wisbech area is renowned for its apple orchards and strawberry fields. Today the Fens are the centre of Britain's bulb and seed industry.*

Ignore the left-hand fork, instead maintain direction to the road ahead.

At the junction turn right along **Wisbech Road** and walk ahead into the village of **Walpole St Andrew**. Turn right at **Kirk Road** and continue to the churchyard of Walpole St Andrew.

*This second marshland church was built between 1420 and 1470, replacing a much earlier church. Inside there is a room thought by some to have been an anchorite cell, and by others a shrine for those about to make the then hazardous journey across The Wash into Lincolnshire. This was how King John lost his jewels, when in this parish in 1216 he went against local advice and tried to make the crossing to Long Sutton. Treasure hunters still search for the jewels today!*

Continue through the churchyard, turn left at the shingle lane and return to the road. Turn right and continue ahead for almost ½ mile to reach **Bustards Lane** on the right.

Turn right along the lane and continue walking this long lane for over a mile.

# 12 Walpole St Peter and Walpole St Andrew

*The tower of St Peter's church can be seen in the distance.*

The lane eventually passes **Bustards Farm** on the left, and then bends to the right. Continue along the lane to reach a T-junction.

④ At the junction turn right and walk ahead towards **Walpole St Peter**, passing pretty cottages and gardens. At the next T-junction, with glasshouses ahead of you, turn right onto **Chalk Road** and, after about 75 yards, look for **Walpole Water Gardens** on the left. On leaving the gardens turn left along the road, passing several houses, as the road bends to the left to rejoin **Church Road**. Continue ahead to return to the start of the walk.

*St Peter's church known as the 'Queen of the Marshlands'*

## Place of interest nearby

The unusual **African Violet Centre** lies a short distance away in the parish of Terrington St Clement. It is signposted just off the A17. Founded by a rector of the nearby church with an abiding interest in African violets, this centre is now recognised as something special with its award-winning collection of these plants in a rainbow of colours. Entry is free and the Centre is open each day throughout the year, except Christmas Day, Boxing Day and New Year's Day. Telephone: 01553 828374.

## Drive and Stroll

# 13 Pentney Priory

*The abbey gatehouse near the start of the walk*

**Distance:** 3¼ miles
**Terrain**: Flat footpaths and farm tracks
**Map**: OS Landranger 132 North West Norfolk, King's Lynn & Fakenham (GR TF702121).

### How to get there

Turn off the A47 at Common Lane, signposted Pentney Lakes, 1¼ miles east of East Winch. Continue for just over 2 miles, passing Pentney Lakes. Ignore the turning to the left and continue until the road bends right, signposted 'Narval Fish'. Go straight ahead, off the road, down the rough track to reach the grassed area signposted 'Car park for Abbey ruins'. **Parking:** In the grassed area to the left of the gatehouse, as directed.

# 13                                                               Pentney Priory

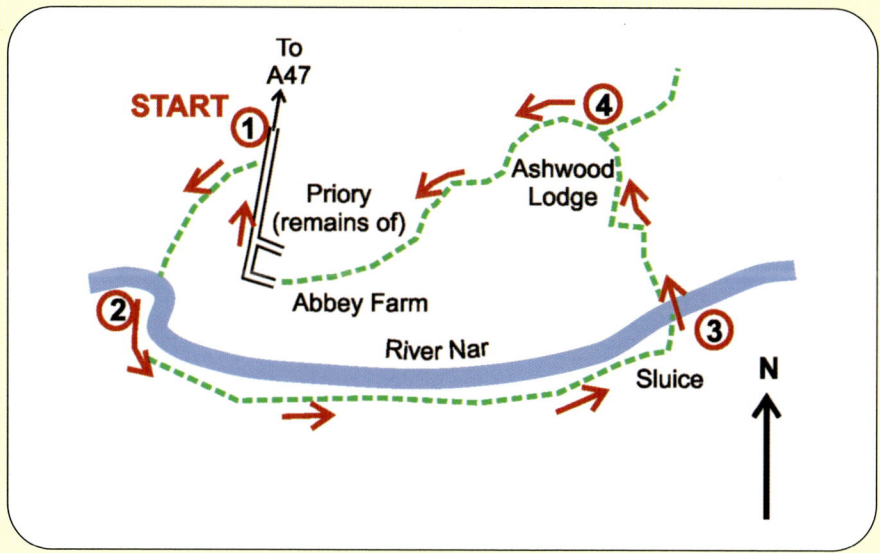

## Introduction
**This stroll starts** at the remains of a once magnificent priory, then follows the peaceful River Nar, using part of the Nar Valley Walk before traversing farmland paths and lanes on its return route. The River Nar, which flows into the Ouse at King's Lynn, has given its name to the walk wending its way from King's Lynn to East Dereham.

## Refreshments
The **Carpenter's Arms** at East Winch can be reached by returning to the A47 and turning left, where it can be found on the right. It is open each day, serving home-made pub food from 12 noon to 2 pm and 6.30 pm to 9 pm. There is also a Sunday carvery available. This free house has a friendly atmosphere and in summer there is a beer garden to enjoy. Telephone: 01553 841228.

## THE WALK

Walk to the right of the gatehouse and after about 30 yards turn right at the public footpath sign.

The Augustinian priory here was founded by the Norman noble, Robert Bigod, in the 12th century and it flourished until the reign of Henry VIII, when it was closed. Handsome stone buildings once stood here and at a visitation in 1492, the priory was said to be the

63

# Drive and Stroll

*most efficient in the country. The great, solid, late 14th-century gatehouse, now in private hands, is all that remains today.*

Continue on the path going slightly downhill. It is joined by another from the left and becomes indistinct, but the wooden footbridge for which you are aiming, is clearly seen ahead.

↳ ②

Cross the bridge over the **River Nar**, then turn left following the river as it wends its way.

*In days gone by, this once busy stretch of water saw cargoes of coal, corn, malt and timber being transported along it. A bone mill harnessed the power of the river to process whalebone from the King's Lynn whaling industry into agricultural fertiliser.*

*Today the sounds of commerce and industry have gone, silence abounds and it is hard to imagine the changes time has wrought.*

Follow the bank of the river, going through metal double gates and a stile. (There was a sign 'Bull in field' on the gate, but we didn't see one!) Continue for 1½ miles to the next iron gate and stile. Go through, still continuing to follow the quiet river on the left. A bridge can be seen in the distance, and just in front of this is a sluice.

*There are beautiful views on this stretch of the walk, both right over the countryside towards Marham Fen, and to the left along the river. Smugglers, who once worked the North Norfolk coast, would row their cargoes of spirits and other goods up the River Nar.*

↳ ③

On reaching the sluice, walk to the right of it, then turn left crossing over the bridge and continue straight ahead on the concrete track. Pass the post with N.C.C. bridle route marked and continue to follow the lane. After 30 yards turn left, then after a further 30 yards turn right. Continue ahead with an excellent view of **Pentney church** in the distance.

*It was in the grounds of St Mary Magdalen church that some rare Anglo-Saxon brooches were found in 1977, by Mr William King, a gravedigger. He thought that they were horse brasses of some kind. Four years later a new rector decided to send them to the Castle Museum in Norwich for identification. They were declared treasure trove and their value set at £135,000. Mr King donated £25,000 to the church; the brooches can now be seen in the British Museum.*

# 13 Pentney Priory

*The bridge over the River Nar at point 2 of the walk*

# Drive and Stroll

Follow the track as it goes left about 500 yards later, heading towards farm buildings. Continue ahead passing in front of **Ashwood Lodge** and go through farm buildings, ignoring a turn to the right. Go ahead on the track as it turns through fields; the track narrows and the gatehouse can be seen ahead over to the right. Continue to the metal gate and pass through the stile to the left of it. After 300 yards, turn right through a wooden gate by a large tree. Cross the wooden footbridge and follow the narrow path through the copse of trees to reach the path walked at the start of the walk. Turn left to return to the car park.

### Place of interest nearby

Just a short distance further along the A47 lies the historic port of **King's Lynn**. It has many architectural splendours to admire and explore. Marriots's Warehouse, a lovely building on South Quay, was a rejuvenation project in the area and now houses a discovery centre dedicated to The Wash and its wildlife. Named The Green Quay it is open every day from 9 am to 5 pm; admission is free. Follow the brown tourist signs for South Quay as you go through King's Lynn.

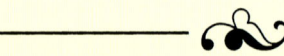

# 14 | Around Blofield and Braydeston

*A pastoral scene at Blofield*

**Distance:** 3¼ miles
**Terrain:** Level lanes and footpaths. There are several stiles on this walk.
**Map:** OS Explorer OL40 The Broads (GR TG335093).

## How to get there

Blofield is 6 miles east of Norwich. Turn off the A47 onto the road as signposted. Continue on this road to the traffic lights by the Kings Head public house, turn into Stocks Lane and then into Church Lane, signposted to Blofield and Braydeston church. **Parking:** On the minor road beside Blofield church.

# Drive and Stroll

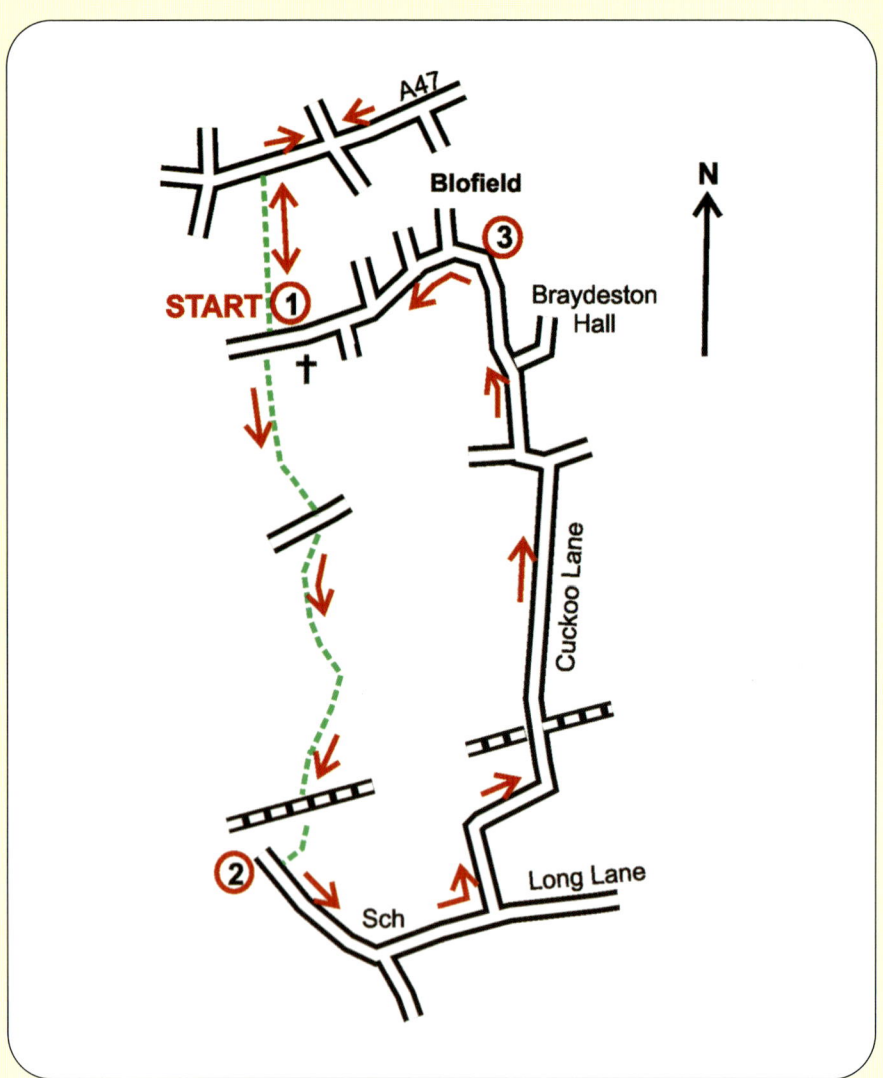

## Introduction
**This easy rural walk** starts from the splendid parish church in Blofield, then leads out to the tranquil setting of Braydeston church, via scenic meadows, often grazed by cattle. The walk returns via country lanes, skirting the villages of Brundall and Strumpshaw, offering superb views of both churches.

# 14 Around Blofield and Braydeston

## Refreshments

Located within the Norwich Camping and Leisure Centre shop, just off the A47 and adjacent to the award-winning farm shop, the popular **Butterflies coffee shop** is open daily for drinks, light lunches, delicious cakes and desserts. Telephone: 01603 717600.

## THE WALK

Go through the wooden gates passing to the right of the church by the public footpath sign and continue ahead.

*The church of St Andrew and St Peter is in a lovely setting, its size reflecting the prosperity of the village as a result of the wool trade. The large churchyard is beautifully kept and it is worth exploring its ancient and atmospheric headstones, before moving on.*

Exit the churchyard by climbing over a stile, then go along the footpath through overhanging trees with a field to the right. After 100 yards the path emerges on an open area of farmland with the footpath clearly visible through the field ahead. Maintain direction, looking back at the lovely view of the tower of **Blofield church**. At the field end climb the stile and continue on the path passing between two wooden posts with a sign saying 'Norfolk County Council, Circular walk'. Walk ahead with beautiful views to the right and the left, towards **Braydeston church**. At the end of the field climb a further stile and pass to the right of the church.

*St Michael's dates mainly from the 13th century, with the addition of its tower in the 15th century. It occupies a lonely site, surrounded by the beautiful Braydeston Hills.*

Continue ahead to reach the next stile at the wooden gate. Climb the stile then turn left again following the circular sign. Look back once more to enjoy the views. Walk on with a wild meadow to the left and fields to the right to the field end. Pass through a small glade of trees to emerge at a cul-de-sac, turn left into **St Michael's Way** and left again on reaching the T-junction to **Long Lane**.

Continue passing very briefly through **Brundall** and **Strumpshaw**. Just after passing **Stone Road** on the right, turn left along **Cuckoo Lane**, with a cream-coloured house on the right. Go ahead for over ½ mile, passing **High Noon Farm** on the left to reach a T-junction.

69

# Drive and Stroll

*The path leading across the fields to the church of St Andrew and St Peter*

There are views of both Blofield and Braydeston churches as you walk this lane.

Turn left at the junction then first right, following the lane to the end. Turn left to arrive back at the start of the walk.

If you wish to visit Butterflies coffee shop by foot, take the footpath directly opposite the church. At the end of this, turn right along the road. Pass by the Blofield sports pitches. Opposite the old milestone on the left, you will find the entrance to the camping and caravan shop. To visit by car, return to the main road and turn right along it.

## Place of interest nearby

**Strumpshaw Steam Museum** has engines, lorries and working beam engines all powered by steam. In addition there is a narrow gauge railway, mechanical organs and a fairground carousel. Steam engine rallies are held during the summer months.

To visit, return to the traffic lights and crossroads, turn right, passing the Norwich Camping Centre mentioned earlier, ignore the fork to the A47 and continue ahead on the narrow lane following the brown tourist signs. Opening times vary during the season. Telephone: 01603 714535.

# Barton Bendish

## 15 | Barton Bendish

*The gentle path through the open fields*

**Distance:** 3½ miles
**Terrain:** Undulating footpaths and country lanes
**Map:** OS Landranger 143 Ely & Wisbech (GR TF714056)

### How to get there

Barton Bendish is 2 miles off the A1122 between Swaffham and Downham Market. **Parking:** On the minor road outside the Spread Eagle public house.

# Drive and Stroll

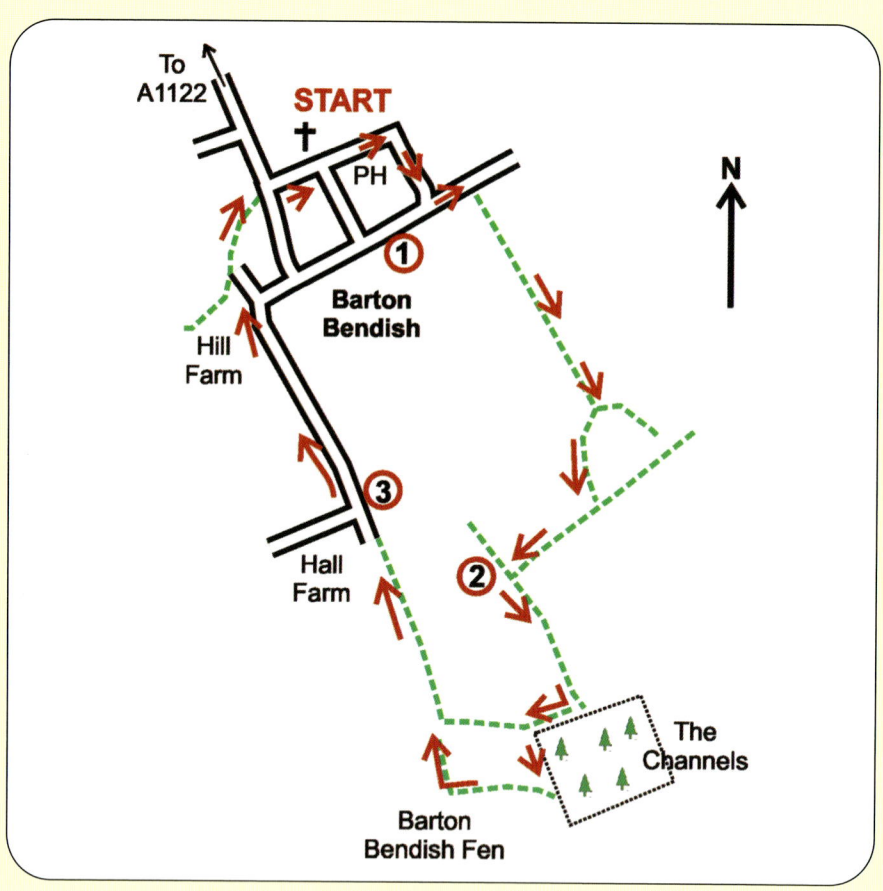

## Introduction
**This wonderful walk** in an unspoilt 'hidden' part of Norfolk embraces the tranquil village of Barton Bendish and its lovely surrounding countryside. The quiet lanes, footpaths and fields are swathed in wildflowers and heavy with butterflies during the summer months. The tranquillity is interrupted occasionally by the roar of a jet aeroplane from nearby RAF Marham, a reminder of the outside world. Barton Bendish attracted a lot of attention in 1920 when it was called 'the loneliest place on the face of the earth'! This was after George Blake was summonsed for infringing the agricultural minimum wage rates. In his defence it was said that the village was so remote that Government orders were unknown! This defence was rejected, but Barton Bendish today remains a peaceful and delightful village.

# 15 Barton Bendish

## Refreshments

The **Spread Eagle freehouse and restaurant** is a place where you can let the world go by as you savour the excellent menu on offer and enjoy the welcoming atmosphere created by the owners, for whom nothing is too much trouble. This superb inn is open for dinner every day and for lunch from Thursday to Sunday. We can also recommend the bed and breakfast accommodation for those who are planning a longer stay in the area. Telephone: 01366 347995.

## THE WALK

With the **Spread Eagle** behind you, turn left. Walk to the end of the lane, then turn right in front of **Avenue House** and continue on the path.

*Note the plum-coloured doors of many of the cottages in the village. In 1992 Count Padulli, an Italian, purchased Barton Bendish Hall and Estate, he then bought back some properties in the village previously sold off. These properties now have the distinctive coloured doors.*

Go through the kissing gate and turn left. After 50 yards cross the tarmac lane and continue ahead at the yellow marker sign 'Norfolk County Council Public Footpath'. In summer, you may see Comma butterflies on this part of the walk.

At **Chapel Lane** turn right, passing the Wesleyan chapel on the left, built in 1875. Continue to the T-junction and turn right. After a short distance turn left at the footpath between two plum-coloured posts. Follow the path, passing a small copse of trees, then at the path junction turn right. The views on this part of the walk are magnificent.

Continue past the ivy-covered pillbox then turn left at the T-junction of paths to arrive at a wood. Ignore the yellow marker sign to the left and take the track to the right. Continue on the track as it bends between the trees. Maintain direction, initially with the wood on your right and then open fields, going slightly uphill to arrive at a minor road.

*On 16th May 1867 Benjamin Black, a woodsman from Barton Bendish, was found dead in Leys Wood, seen in the distance on the left. His nephew, Hubbard Lingley, had shot him, seemingly after a falling out. Lingley has the distinction of being the last man to be publicly executed outside Norwich Castle on 26th May 1867, just ten days after the crime.*

# Drive and Stroll

*Comma butterflies are a common sight around Barton Bendish*

↳ ③

Continue ahead to re-enter **Barton Bendish** village, then as the road bends to the right take the path ahead and turn left along the narrow lane to reach the redundant **church of St Mary**.

*The key-holder to the church lives nearby in a house with a beautifully kept garden. Originally there were three churches in Barton Bendish: St Andrews, All Saints and St Mary's. The parish church of St Andrew is thought to have been the first of the three churches to be built. All Saints was demolished in 1788 and its Norman doorway was reused in St Mary's. The church roof was removed in 1976 and was thatched as part of restoration work.*

Leave the churchyard by the exit gate on the far side and continue ahead passing paddocks on the right. At the crossroads go ahead to **Church Lane** to visit **St Andrews church**. After viewing the church, walk ahead to return to the start.

## Place of interest nearby

The National Trust property of **Oxburgh Hall** is only 4 miles south on minor roads from Barton Bendish. This glorious, moated property is open from March to October, with restricted opening from November. The decorated hall at Christmas and the snowdrops in early spring are magical. Telephone: 01366 328258.

# 16 | Rockland St Mary

*The path at Rockland Short Dyke*

**Distance:** 4 miles
**Terrain:** Level riverside footpaths and minor roads
**Map:** OS Explorer OL40 The Broads (GR TG327047)

## How to get there

Rockland St Mary is 6 miles south-east of Norwich. It is reached by a minor road signposted 'Bramerton and Rockland St Mary' off the A146 just south of Norwich. **Parking:** In the public car park next to the Staithe.

# Drive and Stroll

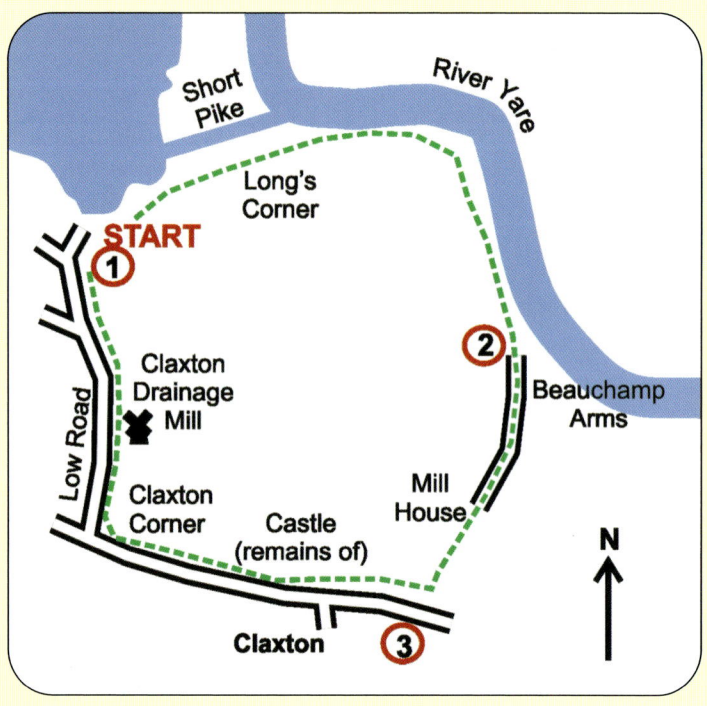

## Introduction
**This pleasurable stroll** takes you by Rockland Broad, known as the Wherry Graveyard, and its bird hide, then alongside the river with its views of wind pumps and wildlife. Meadows, dykes and grazing cattle all add to the delight of this walk. The return along a narrow country lane offers a tantalising glimpse of Claxton castle.

## Refreshments
The **New Inn** is opposite the Staithe car park. It is open seven days a week and is highly recommended. It welcomes walkers, offers a good menu and, in winter, there is a lovely log fire! Telephone: 01508 538403.

# 16 Rockland St Mary

## THE WALK

At the **Staithe** follow the footpath on the left, signposted 'Wherrymans Way'.

*The Wherrymans Way is a long-distance path running for 35 miles from the train station in Norwich to that in Great Yarmouth. The project includes an 800-metre easy access path alongside Rockland Broad. There are good views of the Broad on the left along this path.*

Go ahead on the path, passing through two gates and continuing to the bird watching hide. There is a superb view of the broad from this, so do go inside.

*The remains of several wherries lie beneath the waters of the Broad. They can sometimes be seen at low tides. They are the result of boats sunk on the Broad as wartime defences and they have led to the 'Wherry Graveyard' title.*

Continue along the path to **Rockland Short Dyke**. Turn right keeping the water on the left, then continue ahead to arrive at the **River Yare** and turn right.

*On the opposite side of the river is the chimney of an old steam drainage pump installed by the Proctor Beauchamp family. Visible over to the right is Cantley sugar beet factory.*

Follow the riverbank path passing an electric pump house to arrive at the **Beauchamp Arms**.

*The Proctor Beauchamp family owned land on both sides of the river, including the area where the ferry once operated across this stretch of the River Yare. There were several ferry crossings along the Yare. The only vehicular ferry left in operation is sited at Reedham, further down river.*

Turn right away from the river with the watercourse now on the left and walk ahead through the meadows. Maintain direction along the track ahead, **Mill Lane**, to reach a minor road and T-junction.

Turn right and continue ahead past **The Warren**; this award-winning terrace of houses, was designed by Taylor and Green for Loddon District Council. Go ahead passing cottages and farms as well as **Claxton castle**, clearly seen to the right from the lane.

*Claxton castle was built in the early 14th century for Sir William de*

77

# Drive and Stroll

*Moored up near the Beauchamp Arms pub*

*Kerdiston, who fought at Crecy and Poitiers during the Hundred Years' War.*

Maintain direction to arrive back to the start of the walk.

## Place of interest nearby

The **Ted Ellis Nature Reserve** on Wheatfen Broad is a wonderful reserve and home to the rare Swallowtail butterfly. Ted Ellis was a naturalist of national repute who devoted a lifetime to Natural History and worked to preserve this important site, which is now recognised as a Site of Special Scientific Interest. A remote pair of marshmen's cottages became his family home for 40 years and can be seen near the entrance to the reserve.

To visit the reserve, turn right from the Staithe car park and then right again along the narrow lane to Surlingham, where the reserve is signposted. It is also possible to walk to Surlingham using the footpath, a distance of approximately 1 mile. It is free to enter and is open 365 days a year.

# 17 | Hingham and Hardingham

*The market place at Hingham*

**Distance:** 5 miles
**Terrain**: Level lanes, footpaths and permissive paths
**Map**: OS Landranger 144 Thetford & Diss, Breckland & Wymondham (GR TG022022)

## How to get there

Hingham is situated on the B1108, 14 miles west of Norwich. **Parking:** On the Fairlands, an area of open greens by the crossroads opposite the parish church.

# Drive and Stroll

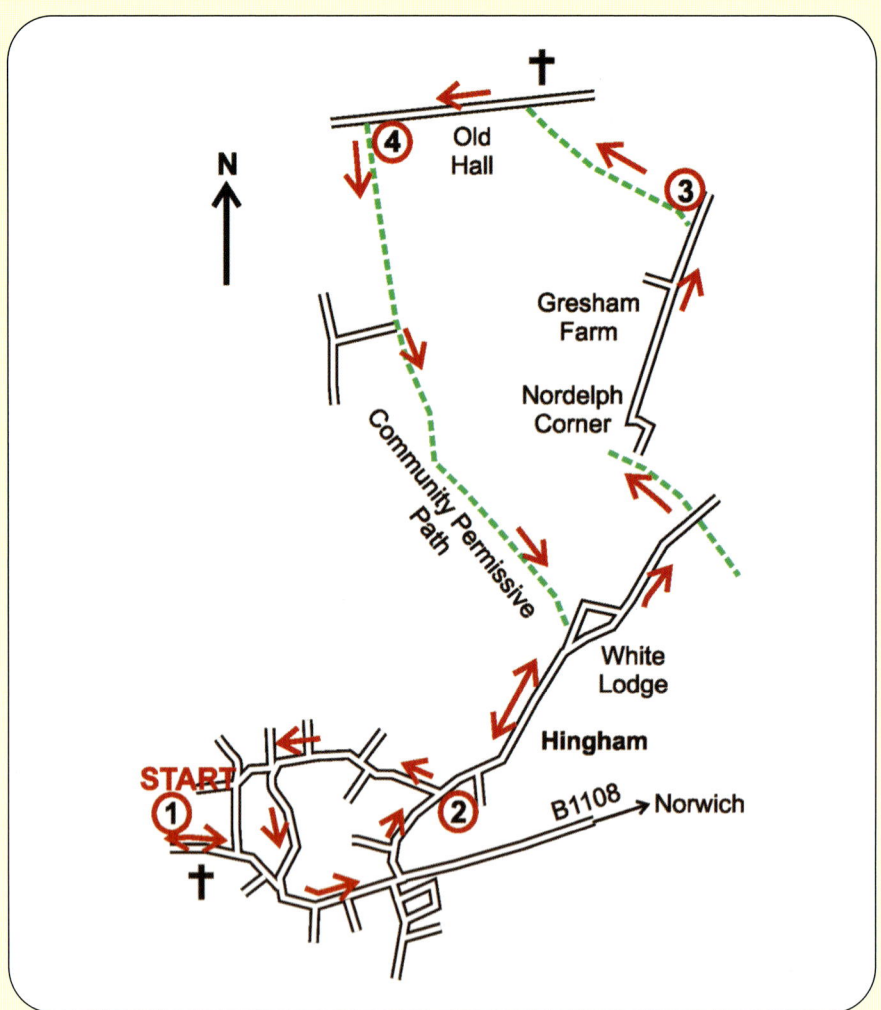

## Introduction
**This is a pleasant walk** around the countryside surrounding the most attractive village of Hingham, leading to a picturesque church and rectory on the outskirts of Hardingham. It returns to Hingham via a permissive bridleway. Hingham village has a wealth of Georgian architecture and an imposing 14th-century church to explore. Inside the church there is a bust of Abraham Lincoln, the 16th President of the United States. His ancestor, Samuel Lincoln, emigrated to Massachusetts in 1637.

# 17 Hingham and Hardingham

## Refreshments
**Lincoln's Tea Shoppe** is a super teashop. It is open all year from 9 am to 4 pm, and serves a very sought-after roast lunch on Sunday; on Friday and Saturday evenings it transforms into a bistro from 6 pm to 9 pm. Telephone: 01953 851357.

## THE WALK

From the **Fairlands** return to the main road and turn left along it, **Church Street**. Continue ahead through the **Market Place** and out through the village to reach a turning to the left, (opposite Bear Lane), signposted to Hardingham and go left along it.

*There is an amazing number of fine Georgian buildings in Hingham, especially around its market place. This stems from its popularity as a fashionable spot during the 18th century, so much so that it became known as Little London; one of the houses still has that title. The village sign at the Market Place commemorates those who emigrated in the early 17th century and founded Hingham in Massachusetts, U.S.A.*

At the T-junction turn right into **Hardingham Road** and continue, passing **White Lodge Farm**, for almost one mile to reach the turning to **Nordelph Corner**. Turn left here, then take the turning to the right following the road as it turns left and then right. Maintain direction along this narrow country lane for nearly three-quarters of a mile then look for the green lane on the left. (The footpath sign is several yards from the start of the green lane, but there is a corresponding footpath sign on the other side of the lane).

Continue on the narrow green lane to reach a wide path and turn right to the country lane ahead. Turn immediately right again and cross to the long drive directly ahead to **St George's**, the parish church of Hardingham.

*Standing next to this isolated church is the beautiful cream-coloured rectory. Side by side they appear to have stepped out of the pages of a Jane Austen novel! The key to the church is held at the next door rectory. Walking up the drive to the church is to step back in time, it is a beautiful building. There are touching memorials to those killed in battle inside the church, and, outside, the graveyard is immaculately cared for.*

81

# Drive and Stroll

From the church return to the lane and turn right along it, passing **Old Hall Farm**.

Look for an unmarked wide green path on the left, with a hedge on the right leading towards a line of trees. (N.B. This new path does not appear on the OS map).

*The path is part of a circular permissive bridleway and conservation walk in this area. The wide grass strips are provided under the Countryside Stewardship Scheme, whilst hedgerows across the farm are being managed to improve the local environment.*

Continue on this path for over 1 mile until it eventually emerges onto **Hardingham Road**, close by White Lodge, passed earlier on the walk. Turn right along the road and maintain direction, this becoming **Hardingham Street**. Continue past several attractive houses with pretty gardens, then turn left into **Bond Street** passing the Dutch-gabled Mansion House with its 17th-century chequered brickwork. Turn right at the end of **Bond Street** onto **Church Street** and walk back to the church and the start of the walk.

*The 120-ft high tower of the parish church of St Andrew's dominates the scene. Inside the church is a permanent display of the links this village has with America, and the Lincoln family.*

Hardingham church, seen from across the fields

## Place of interest nearby

The **Mid Norfolk Railway** runs next to the village of Hardingham. This volunteer organisation has restored 11 miles of the old railway line from Wymondham to Dereham, and has plans for expansion. There is access to the line on either side of Hardingham, at Thuxton or Kimberley Park stations. Special events take place throughout the year. Telephone: 01362 690633; talking timetable 01362 668181.

# Kenninghall

## 18 | Kenninghall

*West Church Street, near the start of the walk*

**Distance:** 2¼ miles
**Terrain:** Footpaths and lanes with slight inclines
**Map:** OS Landranger 144 Thetford & Diss, Breckland & Wymondham (GR TM037862)

### How to get there

Kenninghall is signposted off the A1066, Diss to Thetford road, 4 miles north of South Lopham. It is 6 miles south-west of Attleborough and 4 miles east of East Harling. **Parking**: Available in the Market Place.

# Drive and Stroll

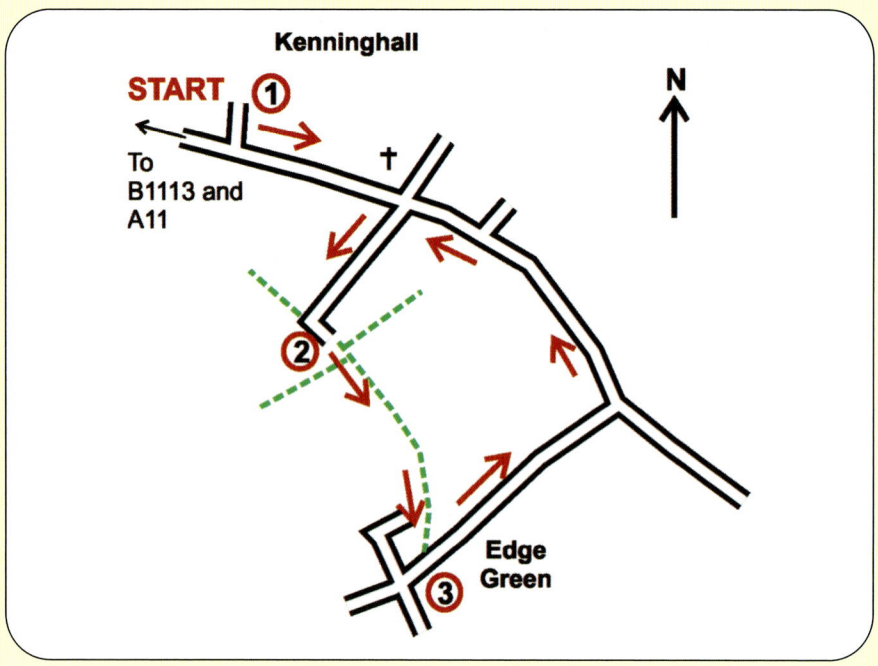

## Introduction
**Kenninghall, a charming Norfolk village** in a conservation area, is noted for its historic buildings. It derives its name from the Saxon *Cyning* signifying king's house or hall. At one time the seat of Boudicca, queen of the Iceni tribe, its distinguished connections were furthered by the Duke of Norfolk, who had a residence here. It continued through the Tudor dynasty when, in 1578, Elizabeth I made a Royal Progress through East Anglia. She stopped at Kenninghall Place, about 3 miles east of the village today. This stroll begins at the Market Place, moves on to the 21st century in the shape of the woodlands of the Kenninghall Lands Trust, before returning via the parish church and picturesque streets to the start.

## Refreshments
The **Red Lion** public house in Kenninghall has received many awards in recent years, following its re-opening in 1997 after a long period of closure. Reputed to be about 400-years-old and licensed since 1722, the now carefully-restored building boasts a very rare 'snug' and original fireplace. It has a well-deserved reputation for good food and is featured in the CAMRA real ale guide. Telephone: 01953 887849.

# 18 Kenninghall

## THE WALK

From the **Market Place**, turn into **West Church Street**. Continue uphill towards the church passing the fine Church Farmhouse with its pargeting. Turn right at the footpath sign by the **Red Lion public house**, this is **Red Lion Lane**, follow the path downhill and cross a wooden plank bridge.

Turn left at the junction of paths by the footpath sign and continue ahead, ignoring the stile to the left to reach Kenninghall Wood and information board.

*In the late 1980s, parish concerns at the loss of trees, woods and hedgerows in the area prompted increasing activity by local residents to reverse this trend, including, in 1999, the planting of Kenninghall Wood, a community wood and orchard. The opportunity to add to this by the purchase of adjoining land culminated in the establishment of the Kenninghall Lands Trust in 2002 and the eventual planting of Hemp Meadow Wood. The interpretation boards give more details of the project and its planting.*

Take the left-hand fork in the path beyond the interpretation board and continue left at the next junction, following the path, then go right by the willow shelter.

*The unusual shelter at Hemp Meadow has been constructed by volunteers using sedge from the nearby Redgrave and Lopham Fen.*

Go ahead passing a handily-placed bench to arrive at the metal gates. Go through the gates to the narrow lane and turn left onto **Heath Road**.

Walk ahead to the T-junction and turn left again onto **East Church Street**. Continue ahead going slightly uphill to reach the parish church.

*Along this section of the stroll there are some fine medieval houses and very pretty cottages to be seen. The architecture is resonant of much of the county of Suffolk across the border, only a few miles to the south.*

Continue passing the church on the right and the **Red Lion public house** on the left.

*The parish church of St Mary sits on the high ground above the road. Over the north door is a set of arms*

# Drive and Stroll

*The award-winning village pub*

to Charles I, considered to be one of the finest in Norfolk, whilst the tympanum bearing the royal arms of Queen Elizabeth I, is one of only four sets in East Anglia.

Walk downhill and turn right into **Back Lane**, following the lane to arrive back at the **Market Place** and the start of the walk.

### Place of interest nearby

**Banham Zoo**, 2 miles to the east of Kenninghall and very well signposted, stretches over 35 acres, with more than 1,000 animals. It has conservation programmes in place for various species and is open daily from 10 am. Telephone: 01953 887771.

# 19 The Pulhams

*Some of Pulham Market's charming cottages*

**Distance:** 4 miles
**Terrain:** Level roads and lanes
**Map:** OS Landranger 156 (GR TM212853)

## How to get there

The Pulhams are on the B1134, 2 miles off the A140, the Norwich to Ipswich road. They are 3½ miles south of Long Stratton and 10 miles north-east of Diss. **Parking:** There is car parking opposite the Londis village shop on The Street in Pulham St Mary.

# Drive and Stroll

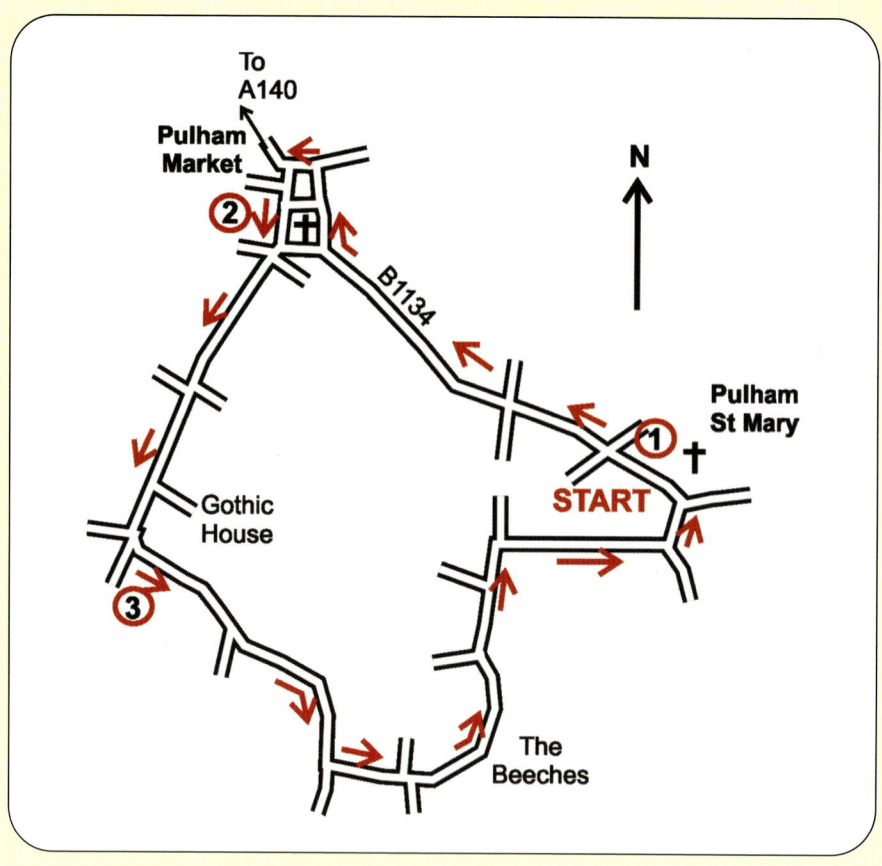

## Introduction
**This stroll linking** the two villages of Pulham Market and Pulham St Mary is a real delight. Using paved roads and tarmac lanes, it is an ideal all-seasons stroll. Beginning at Pulham St Mary, the route takes in a fascinating historic building, before passing through lovely countryside to reach Pulham Market. A circuit around the large green of this quintessential English village affords a closer look at the picturesque cottages adjacent to the green. Leaving the village, the route follows quiet lanes with tremendous views over the countryside. Near the end of the stroll is the church of St Mary, whose magnificence indicates that Pulham St Mary was once very wealthy indeed.

# 19 The Pulhams

## Refreshments

The **Falcon Inn** and the **Crown public house** face each other either side of the Green. Each is very welcoming and we can recommend them both. The Crown is open every day, but closes Monday lunchtime. Meals are served 12 noon to 4 pm and 6 pm to 9 pm. Several gravity-served real ales are usually offered. Telephone: 01379 676652. The Falcon Inn is also open daily for home-made pub food and real ale. Telephone: 01379 767268.

## THE WALK

Turn right along **The Street**, with the village shop on the left. After 100 yards you will see the one-time village school, (currently boarded).

*In the 17th century a rich cloth merchant named William Pennoyer bequeathed money to the village school which continued in use until 1988. One of the classrooms was built into the flint Chapel of St James dating from 1402; its presence on this site remains a mystery. The local community project to restore the site was runner up in the highly acclaimed Restoration Britain TV series. Do stop and look at the excellent information panels around the building façade.*

Continue along the road using the pathway, moving into open countryside with encompassing views. Soon **Pulham Market** can be seen in the distance.

*It is difficult to imagine that in the Second World War huge airships used to take off from a nearby airfield to attack German shipping. They were known as the Pulham Pigs and some were over 600 ft long.*

On reaching **Pulham Market** turn left onto a path beside the **Crown Inn** to visit the church of St Magdalene, the village was formerly known as Pulham St Mary Magdalene.

*The church underwent much restoration by the Victorians and there is a wealth of high-quality glass of differing styles to admire. The church is used today by the Pulham Orchestra for some of their concerts. Few villages today can boast their own chamber orchestra but the Pulham community chamber orchestra, which meets in the memorial hall, celebrated its 25th anniversary in 2008!*

After visiting the church, return to the road and cross over. With the

# Drive and Stroll

*The Crown Inn on the green in Pulham Market*

chocolate-box scene of thatched cottages on the right, continue on the lane to circle the village green. Follow the lane beyond the cottages then continue along it as it bends left to reach the main street. Turn left, passing the **Falcon Inn** on the left and arrive back on the opposite side of the green, with the memorial hall and village sign on the left.

*The sign depicts the biblical story of Mary Magdalen bathing the feet of Christ, and emblems of what were four local public houses.*

After admiring the beautifully-kept village green and taking a break at either or both of the inns, continue the stroll going along the lane to the right of the **Crown Inn**, the lane is signposted 'Seamere Green 1¼ miles'. Continue on this lane passing the attractive old railway station, now a private home, which still has the signal in the garden.

*This is a reminder of the Waveney Valley Railway. It ran through here from Tivetshall Junction via Harleston, and connected with the East Suffolk line to Great Yarmouth at Beccles. The line closed to passengers in 1953 and finally closed completely in 1966.*

# 19 | The Pulhams

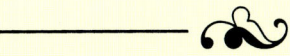

At the T-junction turn left, signposted 'Starston 3½ miles'. Look back at this point for a view of the lovely Gothic house passed on the left just before the junction. Maintain direction for almost a mile on this peaceful lane as it bends round and gives tremendous views of the church of Pulham St Mary, as you stroll to reach eventually the next junction and **Station Road**. Turn left and then almost immediately right. At the lane end turn right back onto **Station Road** and then turn right again off it, opposite **Willow Barn**. From here you can see the top of the parish church. At the T-junction turn left, passing the church on the right and **Church Terrace** on the left, a wonderfully picturesque row of old terraced housing. Continue past the many attractive dwellings to return to the start of the walk.

*The parish church, also confusingly named St Mary's, rises above the street and is equally as grand in looks as that of Pulham Market. It has a superb 15th-century porch with flushwork panelling and outstanding carvings. Viewing is a must!*

### Place of interest nearby

The market town of **Harleston**, 3 miles from the Pulhams, sits on the Norfolk border with Suffolk and is well worth a visit. There is an interesting mix of shops in this popular tourist town and a contemporary art gallery housed in the restored Gurney Bank building, open 10 am to 4 pm Tuesday to Saturday.

# Drive and Stroll

# 20 Thetford

Thetford's colourful iron bridge over the River Ouse

**Distance:** 2 miles
**Terrain:** Level town roads
**Map**: OS Landranger Explorer 229 Thetford Forest and the Brecks, Thetford & Brandon (GR TL884836)

## How to get there

Thetford is off the A11, Norwich to London route. It is also the meeting point for the routes of the A134, the A1075 and A1066. Follow the signs for Thetford railway station (the start of the walk) from whichever direction you are approaching. **Parking:** Free parking in the railway station car park.

# 20 Thetford

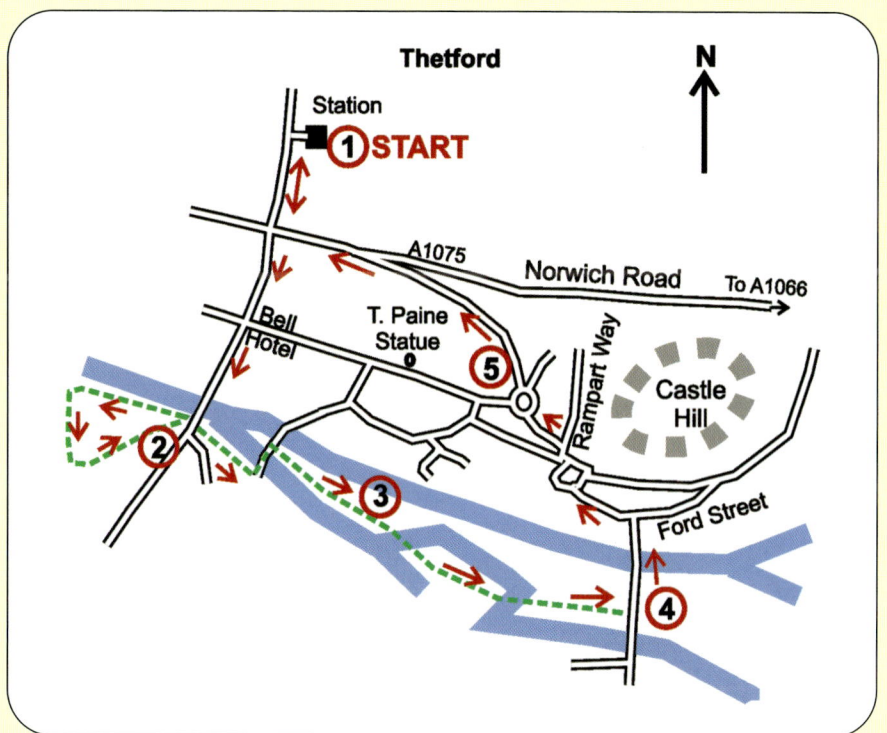

## Introduction
**Thetford is a fascinating place** for a stroll. Starting from the railway station, the route passes along historic streets, a peaceful river and woodland. In recent times many episodes of the TV series *Dad's Army*, still much enjoyed today, were filmed in and around the town. Thetford is clearly proud of its history and shows it in an interesting and accessible way via information plaques, boards and trails. There is much to see and do and this stroll is intended as an introduction to what Thetford has to offer, with options for further exploration.

## Refreshments
The **Bell Hotel** began life as an inn in the 15th century. There are many original features, helping it to retain much of its original character. The hotel has a restaurant and bar, open daily for food and drink, and has a 24-hour front desk. Telephone: 01842 754455.

# Drive and Stroll

## THE WALK

On leaving the station, turn left onto **Station Road**, signposted 'Town Centre'. Continue the short distance to **Norwich Road**, turn left then almost immediately right, and cross the road at the traffic lights to enter **White Hart Street**.

*Here you can see the Thomas Paine Hotel. The great writer and revolutionary was born in Thetford in 1737 in a house that is thought to have occupied this site. Thomas Paine was hugely influential in both the French and American revolutions.*

Continue along **White Hart Street** to the **Ancient House**.

*The Ancient House, a Tudor townhouse, is now a museum with displays telling the story of Thetford and its surroundings. It also houses the death mask of Thomas Paine. Do go in to obtain more information about the town. In 1923, Prince Frederick Duleep Singh donated this museum to the town. His father, Maharajah Duleep Singh, who was a great favourite of Queen Victoria, had been exiled to Britain in 1849 on the annexation of the Punjab in India by the British and lived in Elveden Hall, outside Thetford.*

Walk a little further along the street to the crossroads. On the left stands the **Bell Hotel**.

*The Bell Hotel is renowned as the home to the cast and crew of the popular* Dad's Army *series. Regular gatherings of dedicated fans still take place and participants of the series attending these events stay at the Bell Hotel. The Bell also lays claim to fame as one of the most haunted sites in England!*

Turn left and walk along **King Street** to see the statue of Thomas Paine and then retrace your steps.

*The superb statue, designed by Sir Charles Wheeler, provoked controversy when erected in 1964. The year 2009 sees the 200th anniversary of Paine's death. Many people still find resonance today in his literary expressions, an example is 'the sublime and the ridiculous are often so nearly related that it is difficult to class them separately'.*

You can also turn right by the crossroads, rather than left and walk along **Minstergate** to the **Charles Burrell Museum**.

*This is home to a superb collection of steam traction engines built by the famous Thetford company of Charles Burrell.*

# 20  Thetford

Retrace your steps again to **White Hart Street** and continue along, crossing over a fine cast-iron bridge, constructed in 1829.

 ②

Turn right immediately to walk alongside the **River Ouse**. Stroll along this peaceful stretch to the next footbridge, **Blaydon Bridge**, then turn left away from the river. After 200 yards turn left again along a track signposted 'Town Centre'. Follow the path ahead as it meanders along a grassed area and returns back to the cast-iron **Town Bridge**. Cross straight ahead over the road then, after 200 yards, go halfway across the modern footbridge and turn right, signposted 'Butten Island'.

Continue ahead through very attractive woodland, passing the splendid statue of the Maharajah Duleep Singh on the right. At the junction of the paths, turn right, going over the footbridge, then immediately left signposted 'Nuns Bridge'. Walk ahead through the delightful area of woodland to arrive at the road, this is **Nuns Bridge Road**.

*The British Trust for Ornithology headquarters is based at the Nunnery. The gift of 160 acres of land at Thetford is now managed as the Nunnery Lakes Nature Reserve. There is more than a mile of permissive footpaths to explore, if you have the time. The habitats include fen, open water and Breckland heath. Kingfishers are regularly seen on the water.*

The statue of the Maharajah Duleep Singh

 ④

Turn left, walking with care over the two bridges. At the T-junction turn left into **Ford Street**. To visit the gardens revived by some of the

# Drive and Stroll

local community turn to the right. They are situated in the grounds of **Ford Place** and are open to the public from 10 am to 6 pm, Thursday to Sunday. Continue a little further to view the Norman castle mound which is one of the largest in the country. If you wish to extend your walk, it is possible to walk all around this mound and the site of the Iron Age defences, before returning to **Guildhall Street**.

Otherwise retrace your steps and turn left at **Old Market Street**. Continue to the crossroads and go straight ahead into **Guildhall Street**.

*Look out for the Art Gallery on the left. There are many local arts and crafts to browse through. The coffee shop is open 10 am to 4 pm Tuesday and Thursday through to Saturday.*

Go ahead to the roundabout and straight over to **Earls Street**. If you wish to visit the **Kings House Gardens**, or the plentiful shops, go left at the roundabout and retrace your steps back to this point.

*The Kings House gardens are a popular place from which to escape the bustle of the town. They are open from 8 am to 6 pm or until dusk in winter. There is a mixture of borders, lawns, and specimen trees within these very attractive gardens.*

Continue along **Earl Street** to reach **Norwich Road**.

*You can add to the walk by visiting the remains of the Cluniac priory in Abbeygate, just off Norwich Road. It is open all year and is free to enter.*

Turn left, cross at the traffic lights, and turn left then immediately right to return to the station.

## Place of interest nearby

Over 1 million visitors come to **Thetford Forest** each year. The forest is made up of both broadleaf and pine trees, as well as heathland. At the **High Lodge Forest Centre** there is a café and adventure playground and the forest shop has leaflets, books and information on what the forest has to offer. The centre opening times vary according to the season, but it is open all year at weekends. It is located on the B1107 Thetford to Brandon road. Telephone: 01842 815434.